doug's rooms

doug's rooms

TRANSFORMING YOUR SPACE
ONE ROOM AT A TIME

Douglas Wilson
with Kathleen Renda

PHOTOGRAPHS BY PETER MARGONELLI

Clarkson Potter/Publishers
New York

Copyright © 2004 by Douglas Wilson
Photographs copyright © 2004 by Peter Margonelli except
where noted

Published by Clarkson Potter/Publishers,
New York, New York
Member of the Crown Publishing Group, a division of
Random House, Inc.
www.crownpublishing.com

CLARKSON N. POTTER is a trademark and POTTER and
colophon are registered trademarks of Random House, Inc.

Printed in the United States of America

Design by Jan Derevjanik

Library of Congress Cataloging-in-Publication Data
Wilson, Doug, 1964–
        Doug's rooms : transforming your space one room
at a time / Doug Wilson.
                p.   cm.
        Includes index.
1. Interior decoration.   I. Title.
        NK2115.W812   2004
        747—dc22   2004007455

ISBN 1-4000-5015-4

10 9 8 7 6 5 4 3 2 1

First Edition

ACKNOWLEDGMENTS

I run the risk of writing my autobiography to thank all those I feel grateful to in enabling me to write this book. Don't worry, I won't do that to you. You will get plenty of that later on, like it or not. I must first thank my parents, grandmother, and brothers for their nurturing, torturing, guiding, bullying, and laughing with me. You decide who did what and blame them if you have any problem with me. Seriously, I am grateful for their presence in my life.

To all the designers, contractors, artists, and tradespeople I have learned from and mentored for more than twenty years, I am forever grateful.

To TLC and Discovery Networks for hiring me to design on *Trading Spaces*.

To Denise Cramsey, Tom Farrell, and Banyan Productions, with their devoted crews, for "getting me" and creating episode after episode of my antics and creativity on *Trading Spaces*.

To River Media Productions for launching the first season of *Trading Spaces*, and especially Grace Novinger for spotting me in the April 2000 issue of *House & Garden* magazine.

To Dan Shaw for placing me in the April 2000 issue of *House & Garden*.

To the Triple D's fan club for their never-ending support.

To all my devoted fans who tune in religiously.

To Artgroove artisans for their artistry, support, and humor.

To my management team, Dan Levin and Todd Optican.

To my literary agent, Alice Martell, who had no gray hair when we started this book.

To my advisers, Patric Davis, Chad Boyd, Francis Schultz, James Andrew, and Grey Coleman.

To Alicia Clark for her support and encouragement.

To Dana Scalione for always pitching in to do whatever needed to be done and always looking forward.

To my photographer, Peter Margonelli, who somehow dealt with my insane and ever-changing schedule.

To my cowriter, Kathleen Renda, for channeling me at times and reining me in at others. And lastly to my editor, Pam Krauss, and her team for pushing and challenging me to create the best book I could have.

THANK YOU ALL!!!

DOUGLAS
WILSON

CONTENTS

Introduction   9

PART I: HOW TO DECORATE   16
Proportion and Scale   20
Furniture Placement   26
Color   32
Lighting   40
Managing Clutter   46

PART II: OBJECTS TO INSPIRE   52
Where Do Ideas Come From?   56

PART III: DOUG'S ROOMS   66
Cheeky Tiki   70
French Twist   80
Central Bark   90
Asian Fusion   98
Posh Pucci   106
Heavy Petal   116
Cabbage Patch Chic   126
Beads and Baubles   134
Small Wonder   142
Haute Chocolate   152

PART IV: DO TRY THIS AT HOME   160

Resources   190
Index   192

INTRODUCTION

I know how you live. I've been to your houses, and I've lived that way, too. Sure, I may be a hard-core New Yorker now, with a rent-stabilized apartment and a nearly all-black wardrobe, but my roots are far west of the Hudson. I actually grew up on a small farm five miles from Broadlands, Illinois. We're talking about literally growing up in a cornfield. When someone asks me if I was raised in a barn, I proudly answer "Yes!"

Stylistically, if not geographically, you can't get much farther away from Manhattan than my blink-and-you'll-miss-it rural hometown. Broadlands is smack in the middle of the Prairie State, has a total population of 323, and has never had a stoplight. On our modest —by Midwestern standards, anyway—five-hundred-acre farm, my seven-member family raised soybeans, seed corn, and hogs. Occasionally there were some rabbits, sheep, and chickens around as 4-H projects.

above: PUTTING MYSELF IN FARM'S WAY: THE 500-ACRE ILLINOIS HOMESTEAD WHERE I GREW UP TAUGHT ME MY FIRST DECORATING PRINCIPLE—ORANGE ADDS A ZINGY SPLASH OF COLOR, ESPECIALLY WHEN IT'S A TRACTOR.

CHEZ WILSON WAS A SIMPLE SIX-ROOM house with white clapboards and a green shingled roof. My brothers and I—all five of us—slept in a tiny bedroom off the living room, with bunk beds and a crib for the youngest. Next to the dining room was my parents' bedroom and the only bathroom. It was the ultimate in family togetherness. Who knew that my formative years were preparing me for my current abode, a 500-square-foot pad on Manhattan's Upper East Side?

With a farm to run and little money to spare, my parents didn't exactly put interior design at the top of the family priority list. Practicality was a lot more important than how something looked. Upholstered furniture, whether new from the Sears, Roebuck catalog or bought secondhand, was draped with stain-hiding arm covers and throws. Calendars from the local feed store were nearly the only "artwork" on the wood-paneled walls. Even the one good piece in the dining room, a semi-antique cherry buffet that was a gift from my grandmother, wasn't treated with reverence: my mother thought it was too tall, so she sawed 12 inches off the legs and applied a decorative glaze. (This may explain my own fearlessness toward taking power tools and paint to homeowners' "prized" possessions.)

Over the years my family added onto the house two or three times. There was no grand plan and no great attention to architecture, just a contractor friend who occasionally helped my father with the construction. My dad would say, "Let's add a few bedrooms here and a family room there," and they would go to it, adjusting the roofline accordingly and working without a blueprint. Always thrifty, we built one addition using salvaged wood from a barn we had torn down years earlier. The barn's enormous structural beams became the exposed ceiling and wall beams in the new family room; one of the barn doors was repurposed as a door to the storage space under the stair landing, and the barn siding we turned into paneling, wainscoting, chair rails, and even bookcases. The whole effect was rustic and practical, with a touch of sophistication and lots of honest comfort. It was beautifully done, all 13 rooms and 2,500 square feet of it. The high quality was mainly thanks to one of my uncles, a head carpenter at the nearby University of Illinois, who pitched in with his woodworking expertise. My brothers and I occasionally lent a hand, too, and by the time I left for college I was pretty skilled with a jigsaw and a hammer.

While I was a voice major at the University of Illinois, I dabbled a bit in interior decorating, helping a local artist/interior designer on weekends. My first full-fledged decorating project: covering the walls, ceilings, and floors of my fraternity room at the Acacia house

1. AN AERIAL PHOTOGRAPH SHOT IN THE MID-1950S INCLUDES A VIEW OF THE FARM'S ACREAGE. WHO KNEW THEY HAD AIRPLANES BACK THEN? 2. THE WILSON CLAN, AKA FREE FARM LABOR, LOOKS PICTURE PERFECT IN THE LATE 1970S: MY MERCILESSLY TEASED YOUNGER BROTHER, JOHN, SITS NEXT TO MY MOM, JOYCE, AND DAD, TOM; THE REAR GUARD, PROBABLY PLOTTING SOMETHING SEMI-ILLEGAL, INCLUDES (FROM LEFT), ROSS, MARTY, ME, AND PAUL. 3. TAKING THE CAKE ON MY EIGHTH BIRTHDAY. CONTRARY TO THE BICYCLE DEPICTED IN ICING, I DIDN'T RECEIVE THE MUCH-HOPED-FOR SCHWINN—AND I'M NO LONGER BITTER ABOUT IT. REALLY. 4. AN ARTY BLACK-AND-WHITE COMPOSITION—CHECK OUT THE ANGLED-CAMERA TECHNIQUE!—OF THE HOUSE I GREW UP IN, CIRCA 1955. SOMEHOW, I DOUBT THE CONVERTIBLE WAS MUCH USE WHEN IT CAME TIME FOR PLOWING. 5. FIELD OF DREAMS: MY PATERNAL GRANDPARENTS, ROSELLA AND ARTHUR, DURING THE SUMMER OF 1955. 6. HERE I AM AS A TIGHT END (QUIT SNICKERING) MY FRESHMAN YEAR. 7. I WAS 11 YEARS OLD WHEN I HELPED MY DAD, UNCLE, AND BROTHERS BUILD THE FAMILY ROOM ADDITION, WITH BOARDS FROM A TORN-DOWN BARN. IT REALLY HAMMERED HOME THE IMPORTANCE OF THRIFTINESS. 8. IN A HOUSE WITH FIVE ROWDY BOYS, HANDYMAN EXTRAORDINAIRE DAD WILSON WAS CONSTANTLY FIXING EVERYTHING BUT THE KITCHEN SINK. 9. MY GARDEN-PROUD GRANDMOTHER DORIS, OUTSTANDING IN HER FIELD.

with soundproofing shag carpeting. I also worked on the sets and helped with the stage lighting for the college's drama department, and at local community and professional theaters.

When it came time to leave behind the Acacia brothers and the university, I lit out for Manhattan (after producing my own fund-raising musical, *Road to New York*), to attend the respected National Shakespeare Conservatory and make it as an actor. My parents weren't exactly thrilled, but it was my own money and my own aspiration, and no one could have told me any different. (Sound familiar?)

Like many aspiring actors in New York, I soon realized the bit parts I occasionally snagged wouldn't pay the rent. I took on a host of odd jobs, including dangling thirty stories above the city washing skyscraper windows (talk about trying to get to the top) and making minor household repairs while working as my apart-

ment building's superintendent. I also did carpentry on some small apartment renovations and off-Broadway shows, and pretty soon I was spending more time building stages than acting on them. I liked the work, I was good at it, and I began to build a steady clientele.

My lifeline, and the key to my success, was a *Reader's Digest* do-it-yourself manual. Clients had no idea I was practically a novice. Well, except for that one time I accidentally left the book at a homeowner's apartment, but I convinced her it was purely for reference. Somehow she believed me (hey, I did study acting).

By the late 1980s and early 1990s, I was ranked in a New York City survey as one of the city's top handymen, and I was finally earning some decent cash for my skills. I was also enjoying a rare glimpse into the homes of Manhattan's elite. One of my most intriguing clients was investment banker and multibillionaire Michael Bloomberg, now the mayor of New York City. In his five-story, 7,500-square-foot Beaux Arts limestone mansion I was the on-call handyman, doing everything from hanging pictures and changing lightbulbs to revamping an antique armoire to house a television.

It was in these opulent town houses and penthouses that I first became aware of the decorative painting techniques, like Venetian plaster and unusual glaze finishes, used by the top decorators. On further investigation, it seemed that the decorative painters were doing just as well financially as I was, if not better—but without sustaining the risk of a nail-gun injury. How hard could it be to paint some faux finishes, I wondered,

left: BRUSH WITH FAME: THE AIRY AND ELEGANT ENTRYWAY VESTIBULE I CREATED FOR THE FIRST SHOWHOUSE I TACKLED ON MY OWN (PREVIOUSLY I HAD TEAMED WITH OTHER DECORATORS). ON THE WALLS I PAINTED A CROSSHATCH PATTERN IN A SOFT GREEN GLAZE; ON THE BASEBOARDS, A TROMPE L'OEIL TREATMENT THAT MIMICS LIMESTONE. (PHOTO BY PETER R. PEIRCE)

especially with my background in the arts and in set painting? So I bought a few how-to books on decorative painting techniques and taught myself on the job.

A novice once again but up for the challenge, I found I had a natural knack for decorative painting. Once you understand the basic principles, creativity takes over. Almost overnight, I found myself creating painted finishes not only for my existing clients but for seemingly half of New York's well-heeled residents. I eventually became the city's go-to guy for Venetian plaster, a multistep technique that involves applying layers of plaster and buffing the surface to a high sheen.

It was around then that I started participating in decorator showhouses, a type of fund-raiser in which designers and artists are invited to transform the rooms in a vacant home. People tour the revamped spaces, and the ticket sales are donated to a charity. The biggie is Manhattan's Kips Bay Boys and Girls Club Decorator Showhouse, and I was asked to participate once again in the spring of 1999. The timing couldn't have been worse. I had already committed to doing a Greenwich, Connecticut, showhouse, and as a small business with a staff of four, my resources were limited. But it's a major honor to be included in Kips Bay, and not something you turn down—especially their much-hyped millennial showhouse—so I signed on.

I had about three weeks to glamorize a dark, four-story stairwell, embellished with seventeenth-century-style French plaster detail. For most showhouses, decorators and artists are expected to donate their materials along with their time, and Kips Bay is no exception. This isn't a financial hardship for most well-established decorators, who consider the investment a bargain for the publicity and clients it generates, but I was stretched thin at the time. Labor was no problem but

top: A HIDE TO SEEK: IT LOOKS LIKE BURNISHED LEATHER, BUT IT'S ACTUALLY LAYERS AND LAYERS OF VENETIAN PLASTER THAT I PAINSTAKINGLY APPLIED TO THE WALLS OF THE GUEST BEDROOM IN DESIGNER JAMIE DRAKE'S MANHATTAN LOFT. (PHOTO BY PETER R. PEIRCE)

above: ALLOY THERE! FOR A SHOWHOUSE'S SUMPTUOUS DRESSING ROOM, DESIGNER SUSAN FRANCESCA ORSINI COMMISSIONED ME TO PAINT THIS DRAMATIC DISTRESSED SILVER CEILING. (PHOTO BY PETER R. PEIRCE)

expensive materials were out. So I bought a bunch of inexpensive, 3-inch-round automotive mirrors from a discount store and glued them to the stairwell walls, then added some larger security mirrors I purchased in Chinatown. With brown and orange pencils, I outlined the raised plaster ornaments and drew some whimsical frame motifs inspired by seventeenth-century French architectural details, like pinecone finials. It was fresh, arty, and cheap. The unorthodox—and widely praised—technique earned a favorable mention in the *New York Times,* which led to additional attention in publications such as *Elle Decor* and *House & Garden,* among others. Over the years, my decorative handiwork has appeared in countless New York City abodes, including socialite Brooke Astor's famed red lacquer library (a restoration project) and television journalist Barbara Walters's dressing room.

Eventually, I received a letter from the producers of *Trading Spaces,* who were searching for a—*ahem*—colorful decorator for a new show they were launching on cable's TLC channel.

What *Trading Spaces* viewers respond to in my room makeovers (aside from the verbal sparring I do with some homeowners) is the daring design. Fearless colors, bold fabrics, in-your-face furnishings and accessories—I unabashedly use 'em all, and sometimes all at once. Yes, occasionally my décor has pushed the boundaries of the outlandish and the shocking (the toilet bench was probably ill-conceived), but it's never, ever boring. That's because decorating is a lot like a high-wire act—and if the tightrope walker is only six

above and below: THE MEANDERING STAIRWELL I REVAMPED FOR THE CHICHI KIPS BAY SHOWHOUSE. THE STEPS MIGHT HAVE BEEN STEEP, BUT THE COST FOR REDOING THEM WASN'T: MY NO-FRILLS MATERIALS INCLUDED COLORED PENCILS (FOR OUTLINING PLASTER DETAILING) AND DOLLAR-STORE MIRRORS. (PHOTOS BY PETER R. PEIRCE)

inches off the ground, where's the excitement? Which is what this book is about: nudging you out of your decorating safety zone and toward high-impact design. Within these idea-packed pages, you'll discover that dramatic décor can disguise less-than-perfect rooms, without costing a fortune. You'll realize that bold interiors can be achieved with readily available, inexpensive chain-store furniture and fabrics, not just unique items sold exclusively to the design professionals. And you'll find lots of straightforward advice on tackling common decorating dilemmas, plus irreverent debunking of stodgy design rules. In short, I will let you into my creative mind (scary, I know) and open up yours.

So if you're looking for a chichi coffee-table tome with lots of lush photographs of overdone rooms, $500-a-yard fabrics, and moneyed aristobrats lounging about in 6,000-square-foot villas overlooking Capri, *Doug's Rooms* isn't for you. As for everyone else, what are you waiting for?

Because as my dad used to say when he trooped the Wilson clan out to the fields every summer: "Crops don't harvest themselves. Time to get your butt on the tractor."

above left: A PROMOTIONAL SHOT FROM MY DAYS AS MANHATTAN'S MASTER PLASTERER AND FAUX PAINTER. MY HANDINESS WITH A BRUSH OBVIOUSLY DIDN'T EXTEND TO MY HAIR. **top:** AT *ENTERTAINMENT WEEKLY'S* IT LIST PARTY. MY MOM FLEW TO MANHATTAN FOR THE MAGAZINE'S CELEBRATORY BASH AT THE ROXY. (PHOTO BY PLATZER/FILMMAGIC) **middle:** CUTTING UP WITH A CAKE AND THE *TRADING SPACES* CAST DURING THE SECOND SEASON WRAP PARTY. **above:** TALK OF THE TOWN: BACK IN MY HOME STATE OF ILLINOIS, TO GIVE A LECTURE ON DECORATING FOR THE JUNIOR WOMEN'S LEAGUE IN PEORIA.

PART I

HOW TO DECORATE

DECORATING INTIMIDATES a lot of people. I see the evidence all the time when I'm taping *Trading Spaces* or giving lectures on design. Everywhere I go, I meet homeowners who are stressed out by the whole interior design process. They're short on time, money, and creativity. They're frustrated that their interiors resemble generic rent-to-own showrooms, with matching suites of generic furniture, but they're confused about how to improve them because they aren't exactly sure what the problem is. So they resort to decorating by default.

Maybe you're even guilty of this, too. Tell me if this sounds familiar: For the master bedroom, you buy a headboard, two coordinating nightstands, and a matching dresser. You hang a mass-produced print above the headboard, paint the walls white, and voilà—a finished bedroom. Or you plunk a coffee table in front of the sofa, add two flanking armchairs, hang some framed posters on the walls, shove a fake ficus in the corner and, presto, instant living room. This is the kind of "decorating" that keeps me up at night—and, fortunately for me, keeps *Trading Spaces* on the air.

Doug's Rooms is all about removing the intimidation factor from decorating. Because welcoming interiors that you're happy to come home to every day and that reflect your personality aren't just for a lucky few who are chosen to appear on interior design television shows, or who can afford high-end decorators. Trust me: there are basic principles for achieving high-impact design, and they can be learned easily and put into practice—fast—by *anyone.* I've distilled them into five user-friendly rules that will have a transformative effect on your home and give you the tools to become your *own* designer. Turn the page to start reading about proportion, furniture placement, color, lighting, and clutter control, then flip to page 66 to see how I put them into practice in a variety of spaces.

PROPORTION AND SCALE

size matters

Whenever I attempt to discuss proportion and scale with most homeowners, their eyes glaze over as if I'm a Fermilab scientist deconstructing the intricacies of atom splitting. I keep the definitions as straightforward as possible—proportion is the relationship of one object to another; scale is the relative size of an object —but the response is always vacant stares and dropped jaws. Then I hit on a foolproof way to explain

these crucial decorating principles: I trot out the story of Goldilocks and the three bears. Sure, it seems like a simple fairy tale for the rugrats, but it's actually a detailed, textbook case of scale and proportion that everyone can understand. There's Goldy, puzzling through and trying out furnishings and accessories that are too big or too small, until she eventually hits on the ones that are just right. It's so instructive, it should be required reading for interior design students and anyone decorating a home—especially if the home in question is in a locale where hypercritical, porridge-guzzling blond chippies are roaming around.

Creating a room that feels "just right" for them trips up many homeowners. While recognizing obvious gaffes is easy—a grand piano jutting out of a tiny sunporch, say—more subtle problems are tough to pinpoint, because there aren't as many ironclad rules for scale and proportion as there are for other areas of decorating. Before I redo any room, for example, I have a list of universal design truths that are unchanging: Citrus yellow walls read as energetic, area rugs can carve out separate conversation areas in a large space, and fake flower arrangements are a must-have (if I'm redoing a methadone clinic waiting room, that is).

Proportion and scale aren't as regimented, or as prone to foregone conclusions. Since it's all about objects in relation to one another, it's more intuitive than formulaic, more go-from-the-gut than cerebral. The feng shui industry has made a fortune exploiting this loosey-gooseness by creating strict scale and proportion rules for befuddled homeowners. Which is fine if you want to leach all the vitality out of the creative process and allow your-self to become a decorating drone who has to explain to every guest why there's a mirror hanging over the stove (spare me).

Of course, there's a lot to be said for achieving eye-pleasing scale and proportion in a room by trial-and-error, and learning to rely on your instincts. Within those first few nanoseconds of entering a room we all subconsciously size up the dimensions of the space and the furniture, and know immediately if the room feels "off." The most common mistake that triggers this sensation: furniture that's not in proportion with the rest of the room. Take a master bedroom with soaring cathedral ceilings and a pair of enormous arched-top windows, fairly common in new home construction these days. A space this imposing needs weighty, almost hulking furniture, like a king-size canopy bed and an 8-foot armoire, to counterbalance all that architectural grandiosity. Accessories here should also be large scale: substantial, lush curtains that puddle onto the floor, a table lamp with the circumference of a cistern. Fill a room this gargantuan with wimpy furnishings, and it'll feel like a dollhouse.

The opposite is true for small spaces—usually (hey, I never said this was a gut course, just that you'd be using your gut). Obviously you don't want to cram a sprawling sectional sofa into a Lilliputian living room so that you'll need to walk on top of the cushions just to cross from one side to the other. But petite pads sometimes benefit from the graphic punch of something oversized, like a painting that nearly takes up a whole wall or a massive chaise lounge that fills an entire corner. Seemingly off-kilter pieces like this add much-needed tension in a space that lacks the inherent drama of, say, 20-foot ceilings.

What you want scale and proportion to achieve in any room—large or small—is visual variety. Static spaces are boring. If your space is in dire need of some optical excitement, the following decorating ideas should help open (and entertain) your eyes, and guide you toward creating high-impact spaces all your own:

- Strive to have furniture of three different heights in a room and in equal proportions: tall, like a bookcase or a tree-size plant (please, no bonsais); medium, such as a couch or console table; and low, which can include ottomans or floor cushions. Bedrooms are especially prone to visual monotony because so much of their furnishings fall into the medium or low category. Counter this by increasing verticality with simple, three-foot-tall cylinder vases. Fill a pair with a tall arrangement—curly willow, apple blossom, or forsythia branches are great—and place on the nightstands flanking the bed.

- Fight the fact that most furniture has standardized dimensions: tables and desks are 30 inches high; sofas and loveseats are 36 inches deep; rectangular dining room tables are 34 inches across; queen-size beds are 80 inches long, etc. The upside to all this homogenization is that it simplifies things for retailers and consumers, but the downside is that your rooms are so perfectly in scale that they look weirdly airbrushed. To counter this my-room-was-decorated-by-the-Stepford-wives effect, seek out items that are specially made to be over- or undersize—just make sure they're comfortable, can fit through doorways, and are used sparingly. One piece like this per room is plenty. Or use standard, off-the-rack furniture to create an unexpected juxtaposition of scale and proportion. Turn a straight-backed

wooden child's chair into a funky yet functional bedside table, or mount your mattress on a 5-foot-high elevated plywood platform and mound with frilly linens for a "Princess and the Pea" effect.

- A humongous freestanding floor mirror is a classic of the overscale genre—but it will seriously downsize your bank account. Save cash and get a similar look with inexpensive, stick-on mirrored tiles from a home improvement store. Mount them directly onto the wall, with no gaps between the squares, in a formation measuring as close to 7 feet high by 4 feet wide as you can get. Frame with molding.

- Perch a $3\frac{1}{2}$-foot-high orchid on your toilet tank. If it's fake, I don't want to know about it.

- Work with a photography center to blow up a minimalist still-life image that you've snapped—think Georgia O'Keeffe abstract—until it's at least poster-sized. Frame and hang, or apply directly to the wall with wallpaper paste.

above: PROPORTION AND SCALE CAN BE AS EASY AS CHILD'S PLAY WHEN YOU ADD PINT-SIZED KID'S FURNITURE TO A ROOM. THIS TEENY WICKER LOUNGER DOESN'T DWARF THE DIMENSIONS OF THE LOW-TO-THE-GROUND COFFEE TABLE, AND IT'S A COMFY SPOT FOR RUG RATS—OR CHILDISH ADULTS.

When scale and proportion attack

Talk about a threesome. No matter where I travel in America for a room redo, I consistently encounter the same trio of decorating mistakes involving scale and proportion. Whether I'm in southern Florida, northern Maine, or coastal Oregon, the rooms are always predictably wrong, and eerily identical in their wrongness. (I think there might have been a *Twilight Zone* episode devoted to this phenomenon.) While I can't personally visit all of your residences to point out these gaffes, I've catalogued them below. Chances are pretty good that you're committing at least one—if not all—of the following. Fix them, and your place will look instantly and exponentially better. And I won't even send you a bill for services rendered.

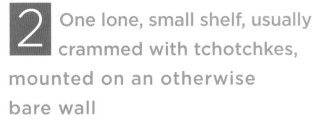

1 Postage-stamp-size artwork hung behind a couch

Ever notice how a Chihuahua standing next to a Great Dane makes the little dog seem even smaller, and the big dog even bigger? That's because side-by-side comparison amplifies an object's perceived size. The same principle applies to your couch. As the largest piece of furniture in your living room, it's going to look even more gargantuan if you place itsy-bitsy art behind it. Keep this relationship in better balance by choosing a print or canvas that's about the same height as the sofa, and between a half and two thirds its width. You can also hang multiple smaller items, as long as their combined total size is equal to the dimensions of the aforementioned single piece of artwork.

2 One lone, small shelf, usually crammed with tchotchkes, mounted on an otherwise bare wall

I've seen this pairing with such regularity that I wonder if it's not a standard feature that's included when you buy a house, like a toilet or a stove. Set adrift on an empty stretch of wall, a single shelf loses any kind of visual impact, and anything you place on top of it will look so inconsequential as to be almost invisible (this may be a blessing in disguise, of course). A solution more in scale with the surroundings: hang three separate shelves, each measuring one third of the total width of the wall, in a slight zigzag pattern. This asymmetrical grouping creates tension by keeping your line of sight slightly off-balance, and its heft holds its own against the visual weight of the wall. Whether two additional shelves can hold all your collectables—I'll take that up in the chapter on clutter.

3 Drapes that end at the bottom of the windowsill

Call it tough-love decorating. I'm on a one-man mission to eradicate ill-proportioned window treatments, and if I have my way, it's curtains for these namby-pamby little half-drapes I see again and again.* Sometimes called café curtains, they're best left to bathrooms and smoky Parisian boîtes overlooking the Seine. Repeat after me: "Partial drapes do nothing for my windows." They look squat, insubstantial, and inconsequential, and are out of balance with the rest of the wall. Ditch the partials for full-length fabric curtains that go all the way to the floor. Want the drapes to have even more impact? Mount the curtain rod well above the top of the window, almost flush with the ceiling. And make sure that the fabric goes *all the way* to the floor.

*Most often in living rooms.

above: NOTHING THROWS A ROOM OFF KILTER LIKE AN END TABLE WITH A LAMP THAT'S THE WRONG SIZE AND SHAPE. CHECK OUT THE PHOTOGRAPHS HERE FOR A QUICK LESSON IN PROPORTION. **1.** THIS SILVER CYLINDER LAMP IS OVERPOWERING. IT'S TOO BULKY AND TOO TALL—ALMOST THE SAME HEIGHT AS THE TABLE ITSELF. PLUS THE DESIGN IS EDGY, NOT CLASSIC. **2.** BETTER, BUT THE HEIGHT IS STILL WRONG. AND THE SPINDLY, SCULPTURAL BASE IS TOO THIN AND INSUBSTANTIAL NEXT TO THE TABLE'S STRONG LINES. **3.** SOLD! THE RIGHT HEIGHT, AND EQUALLY AS IMPORTANT, THE RIGHT WIDTH. THE BOXY SHAPE IS SIMILAR TO THE TABLE'S, AND THE SQUARE DESIGN ECHOES THE PAINTED SQUARES ON THE WALL.

FURNITURE PLACEMENT

making arrangements

When I first started taping *Trading Spaces* I was amazed to discover how many Americans apparently held hoedowns in their living rooms. How else to explain the fact that in home after home all the furniture was shoved against the walls? Of course, I eventually stopped checking for hay wagons parked in the driveway, and realized that there wasn't gonna be any pickin' and two-steppin'—this was just how

people lived. They all told me they wanted their living rooms to be comfortable places for family togetherness and intimate conversations, yet somehow hadn't seen a problem with arranging the seating in such a way that everyone had to shout clear across the room.

Why is it that people don't get this kind of brain lock in other areas of their lives? When you open your clothes closet in the morning, do you wear the first thing you see? No, you think about what you'll be doing that day—lunching with a business client, or running errands—and then choose your outfit accordingly. Maybe you wear a particular item to camouflage the body parts you don't like, and play up those you do. All I'm asking is that you try to be at least half as analytical about furniture placement as you are with your wardrobe.

Before you start cramming a room with furniture, you need to figure out exactly what you'll be doing in the space. Do you need a semisecluded spot for paying bills? What about a cozy nook for reading? Will the kids be doing homework here, or maybe watching television with their friends? (Bathrooms are pretty self-explanatory.) Deciding on a room's functions beforehand will help guide you in purchasing and arranging your furniture. Otherwise, you'll end up trying to retrofit stuff that you bought because you liked it, or because it was on sale, but that doesn't fit the room's game plan. That's the equivalent of wearing a bought-on-the-cheap cocktail dress that was marked down (twice!) to a meeting with your boss. Sure, the dress may have been a steal, but unless you're a socialite, it's not exactly work-appropriate attire.

The next thing you want to do is figure out where the room's focal point is going to be. This is the spot your eye is naturally drawn to, and you'll position the majority of your furniture toward it. Usually it's a major architectural feature—a fireplace, a picture window with a panoramic view—but in rooms without a natural focal point, it can also be something subtler that you've manipulated into visual prominence. A striking piece of artwork, an unusual family heirloom, even a fake mantelpiece can be turned into focal points. Notice I didn't mention the word *television*. Yes, it's the electronic hearth, but as focal points go, the boob tube is a bust—it's squat, unattractive, and unsociable. If you insist on turning yours into a focal point, at least stash it in an armoire or a cabinet with doors, so it can be hidden away when it's not in use.

After you've selected your focal point, you want to position the largest piece of furniture opposite it, at a distance of about 10 feet. Next, angle other seating in the room so it also faces the focal point. Refrain from turning every single chair in the place toward this artificial view—you're not re-creating a movie theater. If your focal point is a fireplace, this usually means your sofa will be situated in the middle area of the room. *Do not panic.* Arranging furniture away from the walls like this is called floating; professional decorators do it all the time to optimize space, and no one has been harmed yet. Yes, you see the back of the furniture, but you paid for that part too, right?

The next step in arranging your furniture is to assemble what I call the intimate areas, which are little rooms within the room. These are the quieter spots where you'll be doing a specific task, and they usually *don't* face the focal point. An intimate area can be as simple as a desk in a corner for working on a computer, or a chaise lounge surrounded by bookcases and a reading lamp that carves out a mini-library. Again, some of these pieces may float, but as long as you're not impeding the traffic flow of the room, *it's okay.*

below: POSITION FURNITURE TO BREAK UP THE EXPANSE OF A LARGE ROOM AND CREATE DISTINCT AREAS. TRUE TO ITS NAME, THIS SECTIONAL SOFA DIVIDES AN OPEN STUDIO APARTMENT INTO SEPARATE SECTIONS FOR DINING AND LOUNGING, A TRICK THAT ALSO WORKS FOR OVERSIZED LIVING AND FAMILY ROOMS.

Problem-o-rama

Homeowners often complain that it's not their furniture that's causing their arranging dilemma, it's the room. Yes, rooms can have flaws, and you need to decide whether you want to work with them or against them. If you have a sky's-the-limit budget, you can move load-bearing walls, cut out additional windows, expand doorways, and raise ceilings. For the rest of us, it's a matter of assessing these problems and disguising them through some clever decorating sleight of hand. Check out the quick fix list below for solutions to the most common floor-plan problems.

An awkwardly positioned closet

Is there a closet right where you want to place a bookcase? Or maybe the closet's doors open onto the area you allocated for a bed? Try transforming the closet into a recessed alcove: Remove the doors, and paint the interior a darkish shade that contrasts with the room's color scheme. Mount shelves from top to bottom, fill with accessories—or better yet, a television—and add a bookcase light for illumination.

An awkwardly positioned window

I hear this complaint so often, I'm wondering if architects aren't deliberately adding this design flaw as a kind of inside joke: try decorating around this, sucker! Windows can be problematic if they're off center, mounted too high or too low, positioned asymmetrically along a wall, or hugging a corner. One of the most effective strategies for counteracting a poorly placed window is to completely surround it with a bookcase wall unit (this may require a custom-built piece); with shelves enclosing it on all sides, the window's prominence recedes and it no longer jumps out as an architectural element.

You can achieve a similar effect by hanging an arrangement of artwork that's the same height and approximately double the width of the window; mounting prints or canvases parallel to the window creates counterbalancing visual weight. For side-by-side windows of unequal sizes, use draperies to create faux symmetry: on the smaller window, use too-big curtains and hardware that match the size of the larger window—your eye will be fooled into thinking it's seeing two windows of the same dimensions.

An awkwardly positioned doorway

Remedy a klutzy door that's jutting into a room by rehanging it so it swings in the opposite direction. Or try removing it altogether and replacing it with a swagged curtain, beading, or even a window blind. You can also use the same artwork-balancing and fake-drapery tricks as described in the window solution, above.

COLOR

color scheming

It's a small world, but I wouldn't want to paint it.
—STEVEN WRIGHT

Crisscrossing the country for *Trading Spaces*, I've detected a bizarre color blight that afflicts a growing number of homeowners: no one uses any. For whatever reason (lethargy? paintbrush . . . too . . . heavy?), the only shade folks seem to have on their walls consistently is white. Or, if they're really daring, off-white.

This nationwide tyranny of noncolor color isn't just bland and boring—it's also the single biggest missed

opportunity for creating high-impact design. That's because the easiest, cheapest way to transform any room is with a gallon of paint.

Of course, deciding upon a room's color palette shouldn't happen by accident, although it usually does. Most people, without any preliminary reconnaissance, beeline straight for the home improvement store's paint chip aisle. There they're accosted by an eye-blistering array of literally thousands of colors. Buying paint should occur only after careful planning and consideration, so start by asking yourself the following questions. Hue knew?

below: AT A CONNECTICUT SHOW HOUSE, AN UPSTAIRS LANDING TOOK OFF TO THE WILD BLUE YONDER ONCE I APPLIED GLOSSY VENETIAN PLASTER IN VARIOUS SHADES OF SKY AND AZURE. (PHOTO BY PHILLIP ENNIS)

How do you want the room to make you feel?

There's a reason we say that we "feel blue," or that someone is "green with envy": color affects our mood. Studies have shown that certain colors can raise or lower blood pressure, aid in digestion and concentration, make us sleepy or more alert. Decide how you want to feel when you walk into a room. Are you after something peaceful and calming, or something invigorating and stimulating? Do you want to encourage conversation and lively debate, or keep things subdued and quiet? Check out the following list for insights into how certain colors can raise and lower your emotional temperature.

Red

Passionate, upbeat, and adventurous, the red family ranges from blackish burgundy to powdery rose. Like the racy lingerie of the color wheel, it spices up ho-hum rooms with red-hot sultriness and sass.

PRO: can add a regal feel—hence the phrase "red carpet treatment"—so it works well with traditional furnishings. Try a high-gloss lacquer red in a small powder room; tomato red kitchen walls plus white cabinets equal a sociable bistro. **CONS:** overpowering in large doses, and agitates anxious types (i.e., "seeing red").

Whites

What, you think I'm going to encourage you to use this shade? You want your walls the color of unbrushed teeth, kiddo, you're on your own.

Blue

Evoking cloudless skies and tranquil seas, this serene, calming, and relaxing shade has universal appeal—it's the favorite all-around color of most Americans (think it's a coincidence we're the country that invented blue jeans?). Blue is amazingly versatile and far ranging, whether it's the vibrant azure of Moroccan tiles or the soft slate blue of Scandinavian interiors.

PROS: Blue produces peaceful moods and contemplation, so try its de-stressing properties in the bedroom or a study. It blends easily into a variety of multicultural decors, and can be partnered with orange for an exotic, contemporary effect or deep brown for a rich, elegant feel. And what else would you use to create a nautical or spa theme in a bathroom? **CONS:** Icy blues can look chilly and clinical. Make them more welcoming by choosing shades of blue with warmer, deeper undertones.

Green

Symbolizing life and renewal, green is simultaneously refreshing and calming. The most common shade in nature, green is a balancer (it's halfway between blue and red on the color wheel) that can harmonize disparate colors.

PRO: Contrary to what Kermit says, it's easy being green. Time seems to move faster in a green room, it's soothing to the eyes, and it promotes healing and rejuvenation. Try soft kiwi green in a bathroom, shocking shamrock in a family room, light celery in a formal dining room. **CON:** Sickly yellowish greens can actually induce nausea, which is why the shade is avoided in airplane and ship interiors.

Orange

Stabilizing and reassuring, orange is autumn personified—think pumpkin patches, falling leaves, Indian corn. Its edgy side complements modern interiors, especially when partnered with Barbie pink or chocolate brown.

PRO: Cheerful and informal, orange is a party-hearty color that encourages lively interaction. Carrot orange stripes can zest up a playroom; tangerine on the recessed walls flanking a bumped-out fireplace is cutting-edge hip. **CON:** Since it increases appetite, it's the default color of most fast-food restaurants. Bright "safety" orange identifies acute workplace hazards—so it's probably not the best choice for a nursery.

Yellow

The most visible color in the spectrum, it's replacing the traditional red on fire trucks. Sunny and happy, it revs up light-deprived rooms—perfect if you have mostly north-facing windows.

PRO: Yellow is said to increase mental alertness. Whether it's tart citrus, mellow mustard, or deep ochre, yellow's flattering, wide-ranging spectrum doesn't have a lemon in the bunch. Perk up dated kitchen cabinets with egg-yolk yellow, or use a solar yellow as artificial sunlight on a windowless bathroom's walls. **CON:** Because yellow is not exactly a restful color, especially if you're prone to mental anxiety—check out van Gogh's frenetic sunflowers—proceed with caution in a bedroom.

Purple

Mysterious, aristocratic, and spiritual, this underused color can transform a room into an exotic sanctuary.

PRO: The color of royalty, purple creates a luxe look with minimal effort. For an elegant 1930s-inspired boudoir, partner violet with shimmery silver accents. **CON:** associated with death and suffering in some religions. Pink-based lilacs are too precious for most rooms—unless you're a preteen girl decorating her bedroom, in which case it's, like, the best *ever*!

What kind of light does the room get?

The intensity and amount of sunlight a room receives can profoundly affect the way a color appears. Depending on the time of day, a color can look either animated or anemic, or somewhere in between. Geography also plays a role. In the tropics, only vivid colors like electric turquoise or yellow can withstand the blinding sunlight without looking washed out. Import those same colors to Iowa and they can look loud and cartoonish, which isn't always a bad thing. And if you live in that part of Alaska where twenty-four hours of daily sunlight is the norm in summer—move.

Determine your room's exposure. If the windows face north, there won't be any direct sunlight and the space will feel chilly; try a cozy red or orange-yellow color to warm it up. A south-facing room is exactly the opposite: it will be flooded with lots of light all day, causing the wall color to seem warmer and look more yellow; cooler shades can help deflect the heat. East-facing windows get all their sunlight before noon, so if you're spending time by them in the morning, you'll need more subdued hues to counteract the glare. Windows that face west enjoy afternoon sunlight, but it will be reddish closer to dusk, and make dark colors appear muddy.

Paint a decent-sized swatch of wall with the color you're considering and observe it under a variety of lighting and weather conditions. Only when you're satisfied that the color performs the way you want should you greenlight a purchase.

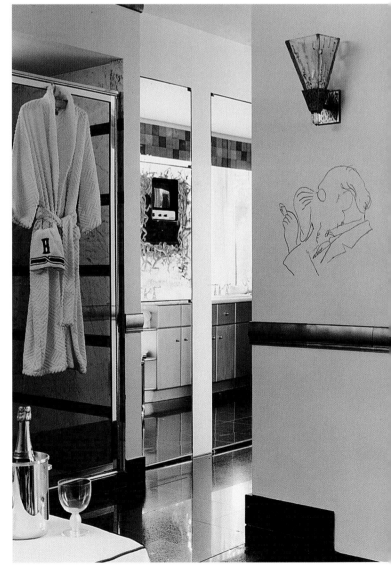

right: WHAT DO YOU DO WITH A LARGE ROOM THAT HAS ONLY A SINGLE, UNDERSIZE WINDOW? LIGHTEN UP, WITH WHITE WALLS AND A WITTY LINE DRAWING BY JEAN COCTEAU—THE APPROACH I USED IN THIS SHOW HOUSE'S MASTER BATHROOM.

What kind of paint should I buy? Or, a gloss glossary

Paint comes in five types of finishes: flat, eggshell, satin, semigloss, and high gloss. Selecting a particular finish might initially seem confusing, but for most homeowners it really comes down to practicality. Just ask yourself one simple question before choosing a finish: how often do I want to scrub this wall? (Of course, if you can sucker your spouse into a lifetime of wall-washing duty, skip this section.) Paint finish differs in wearability and washability—the lower the gloss, the harder it is to keep clean. So painting an easily dirtied room like a kitchen with a flat finish isn't advisable, unless you own stock in Merry Maids. Check out the chart below for a paint primer.

Flat

Has zero shine and a matte, almost velvety appearance. Reflects the least light of any of the finishes, so the color is less intense compared to higher glosses. Can be tough to keep clean as the surface is essentially unsealed. **BEST FOR:** bedrooms, living rooms, and dining rooms. A great disguiser of wall imperfections like pitting and roughness. **NOT SO GREAT FOR:** bathrooms and kitchens. It's so porous it sucks up grease and dirt like a sponge.

Eggshell

Has a slight sheen similar to, well, the shell of an egg. Its low luster gives rooms a warmer glow than flat paint. Very washable. **BEST FOR:** bedrooms, living rooms, and dining rooms. Easier to clean than flat. **NOT SO GREAT FOR:** kitchens and bathrooms, unless you order a lot of take-out food and have a low-traffic powder room.

Satin

A soft-looking finish that's a bit shinier than eggshell. **BEST FOR:** kitchens, bathrooms. Also, doors, window frames, trim, and moldings, because it provides subtle contrast with flat finish walls. **NOT SO GREAT FOR:** hallways, or areas that need frequent touch-ups—the difference in the sheens will be visible.

Semigloss

A popular, all-purpose finish. Long lasting and actually scrubbable. **BEST FOR:** kitchens, bathrooms, kids' rooms, and on cabinetry. The Teflon of paint finishes, it's virtually unfazed by humidity, stains, and wear and tear.

High-gloss

Creates a brilliant, shiny, hard surface that looks almost plasticated. Provides the most intense color of all the finishes. Highly resistant to mildew and moisture, and practically self-cleaning. **BEST FOR:** trim and molding—and professional painters. See the cautions below. **NOT SO GREAT FOR:** walls, ceiling, and cabinets. If they aren't absolutely pristine and blemish free, even the smallest divot will resemble a crater.

Paint, by numbers

Before plunking down your hard-earned cash on a gallon of Prairie Dawn or Mozambique Midnight, it pays to brush up on some paint economics. Inexpensive paint, which runs about $13 a gallon, seems like the better buy compared to premium varieties—which can fetch $30 and up per gallon. But cheaper paint contains less pigment than better-quality versions, which means you'll need more coats to cover the same square footage. Because it's thinner, lower-grade paint doesn't adhere as well to walls, so expect more flaking and crumbling—and repainting. You do the math.

LIGHTING

light up your life

All the world's a stage.
—WILLIAM SHAKESPEARE

In addition to writing history's greatest plays, I'm guessing Billy Shake moonlighted as a decorator. As someone who's toiled behind the scenes of community and off-Broadway theater productions, I know that the stage is a perfect model for real life—especially when it comes to lighting. During a play, when you want to direct the audience's attention to a certain character, you shine a spotlight on the actor, causing

everything else to recede into the shadows. Colored gels over lenses, dim illumination, and strobes create instant atmosphere. Plunging the set into absolute blackness signals a dramatic shift in mood.

These same concepts apply when you're lighting a room, but most folks seem completely in the dark about them. Strategically placed lighting can compound the interest of high-impact design by directing the eye and creating a mood with the flick of a switch. Yet rather than using light as a valuable design component, too many homeowners just flip on the standard overhead fixture that came with the house, switch on a couple of table lamps, and—whew!—call it a day. It's like living in the nineteenth century when Edison first trotted out his new-fangled incandescent contraption, and a bare bulb was the height of illumination sophistication. We've got electricity full-time now, people, and stores devoted entirely to lighting, so there's no excuse for gloomy interiors. These ceiling fixtures are a personal pet peeve of mine; they direct all the light up toward the ceiling, exactly where it's not needed, flatten and dull colors, and cast the room in unflattering shadows. (I won't even dignify the light/ceiling fan combo with a mention.) Remember: proper lighting is as flattering as a face-lift, without all the expense and recovery time. No one looks any younger when they're illuminated by an overhead.

Now that we've established that nothing can hold a candle to a well-lit room, how do you achieve a gorgeous glow? Let's shed some light on the subject with a description of the three basic kinds of illumination: ambient, task, and accent.

left: SHINE A SPOTLIGHT ON STYLE BY CHOOSING LAMPS THAT COMPLEMENT—OR CONTRAST WITH—YOUR ROOM'S DÉCOR. HERE, A SLEEK METAL FAUX BAMBOO FLOOR LAMP ADDS CLEAN-LINED ASIAN SOPHISTICATION TO A FUNKY, ORIENTAL-INSPIRED FAMILY ROOM.

Ambient

Think of this as a substitute for sunlight. It provides the basic illumination in a space, and it's usually the first light you turn on when you enter a dark room. For most people, it's provided by a ceiling-mounted fixture, like a chandelier.

Task

Like the name implies, this is intense light for a specific purpose. It illuminates only a limited area so you can see what you're doing—reading, embroidering, using the computer—without straining your eyes. Task lights should be adjustable and three times brighter than ambient light, without giving off glare.

Accent

These are lights for effect, not illumination. They're used to highlight a picture, a bookcase, or a sculpture. Like mini-spotlights, they're about creating focused drama.

Lighting in every room should always be a proportionate mix of ambient, task, and accent. Don't be stingy when it comes to using lamps and fixtures—most of us are actually living in rooms that are poorly lit, without even being aware of it. To calculate the correct amount of illumination needed for a space, multiply the room's square footage by 1.5; the result is the total number of watts needed to light the room. A 10 × 20 bedroom is 200 square feet and requires a minimum of 300 watts—which means relying solely on an overhead fixture with two 60-watt bulbs isn't such a bright idea. Keep in mind that the older you are, the more you need to crank up the wattage: a sixty-year-old requires almost fifteen times more light to read by than a ten-year-old. Are you beginning to see the light?

Watt's up?

Aside from color, everything pales in comparison to lighting when it comes to transforming the look of a room. Track lighting, sconces, freestanding floor lamps, electrified candelabra, rainbow-hued pulsing orbs—all can change a space dramatically at the touch of a finger. But you don't need a thousand-dollar Murano glass chandelier from Italy to make a bold style statement. These offbeat, affordable lighting solutions will have you seeing things in a whole new light.

- Put every light on a dimmer switch for at-your-fingertips ambiance. Dial down for a candlelight effect, dial up for faux sunlight.

- Turn a ficus tree into a shadow theater. Insert a tiny plant light discreetly behind the trunk so that it faces upward and projects leafy patterns onto the ceiling.

- Christmas lights aren't just for Yuletide. Mass clear string lights in a casual jumble in an unused fireplace, or randomly poke the bulbs through a craft store artist's canvas for instant illuminated artwork.

- Transform light boxes, made for viewing slides and available at photography supply centers, into sly sculpture. Have a copy center print your favorite image onto overhead projector transparency film that you've purchased from an office supply store. Or use transparency film that's inkjet compatible, and print out a scanned photo from your home computer directly onto the film. Mount a trio of light boxes on a blank wall, then attach the tricked-out transparencies using extra-large binder clips.

- Avoid hanging a lone pendant lamp above your dining room table—it's clichéd, and doesn't offer nearly enough illumination. Instead, suspend five identical pendant lamps across the entire length of the table.

- Crack a dozen 15-inch blue and green glow sticks and pop into a clear glass vase during your next party.

- Three words: uplights, uplights, uplights. Shaped like cans of soup, these pint-sized powerhouses throw amazing accent light.

- Go industrial chic with oversize clip-on metal utility lights from the home improvement store. Clamp a half-dozen along a length of vertical plumber's piping that you've attached to the ceiling and floor. To soften the look, lightly sand the lamps with fine steel wool and paint with high-gloss enamel in shades to match the room's decor.

- Bookcase lights aren't just for illuminating your library of hardcover best-sellers. Use these Lilliputian lamps above a dry-erase board, a bathroom mirror, or inside a glass-fronted kitchen cabinet.

Made in the shade

Most chain store lamp shades are practical and charmless—they dutifully shield a naked bulb and diffuse light, but they aren't much of a visual turn-on. Put the fun back in functional by customizing a ho-hum shade with these easy Do Try This at Home embellishments. Since the shades are so ornate, keep the base basic, and remember that illumination decreases as the amount of embellishment increases.

- With a hot-glue gun, (gingerly) apply fluffy white ostrich feathers from a notions store onto a shade. Cover completely, so that none of the shade is visible. Pair with a crystal or Lucite base for instant boudoir glam. For additional luxe, trim the shade with maribou by the yard or mink pom-poms spaced at 3-inch intervals along the bottom of the shade.
- Transform a tall, thin floor lamp into the lighting equivalent of a sixties go-go dancer. Cut 2 yards of double-faced white faux leather from the fabric store into strips that are 2 inches wide and as long as the lamp is tall. Squirt a thin line of fabric glue onto the very top of the shade. Carefully affix the leather strips to the shade—don't overlap—to create a kicky fringe effect. Or substitute a fringe made of stiff fabric or strings of large glass beads, attached with a staple gun to the top inner portion of the shade.
- Hot glue a thin sheet of cork from the home improvement store onto a drum shade for a combo bulletin board/table lamp.

MANAGING CLUTTER

coming to order

Clutter is taking over America. Like some oozing blob from a cheesy sci-fi movie, it's invading homes and seeping into every nook and cranny. It's so insidious and unstoppable, I'm surprised there aren't more victims of clutter like the infamous Collyer brothers. In the late 1940s, the siblings were found entombed in their Harlem brownstone, completely engulfed by more than one hundred tons of junk—including ten grand pianos, fleets of rusted bicycles, and chest-high stacks of yellowing newspapers. Most homeowners

PHOTO BY PHILLIP ENNIS

haven't quite reached that point—yet. But they're inching closer. While taping *Trading Spaces* I've been in homes where off-camera rooms were so crammed with wall-to-wall stuff that our production crew could barely maneuver. I've seen bathtubs employed as makeshift dressers, and a Christmas tree still in the living room in mid-July. Luckily, it was a faux fir. And these were in houses where the folks actually knew visitors were showing up—with television cameras!

It's way too easy to be afflicted with possession obsession in this consumer culture. We're constantly bombarded with images of things we need —or think we need—and as a result our homes are bursting at the seams with accumulated junk. Worse, most of us can't seem to throw away anything. We collect, we hoard, and we cling to things because we feel they have sentimental value. All this oppressive stuff will suck the desire for decorating right out of you, plus make you want to lie down in a darkened room—if only your unmade bed wasn't completely covered with laundry waiting to be folded.

Now, I understand that your possessions are important to you. But there's something you need to hear, even though it's going to further solidify my reputation as a home wrecker with an imperious streak: throw out the crap. Or use a flamethrower if there's one handy (and god knows, there probably is). Just get rid of the clutter. Because even the most beautifully decorated room is going to look like a two-bit rummage sale if it's stacked floor-to-ceiling and wall-to-wall with junk. Lose all the knick-knacks that are littering every available surface in your home. (Trust me: the sell-by date on Beanie Babies is looooong past.) Dump anything that's bro-

ken, stained, shopworn, rarely used, or just plain ugly. You get the point, I'm sure.

Of course, purging your rooms of unnecessary clutter is only step one in organizing your possessions. You also have to create an ordered system for all the stuff you *do* need. Okay, don't start hyperventilating—you're not required to sort your sweaters by fabric content or alphabetize your CD collection by musical subgenres. All you really need to do is designate specific spots for specific items, so you're not hunting for your car keys in the dryer's lint compartment. The goal is to take the decision-making out of organizing and create an efficient home that is calming and streamlined, so you can actually see the interior design.

Tidying isn't traumatic. It doesn't require the services of a $100-an-hour professional organizer, and it doesn't mean just dumping your stuff unceremoniously into milk crates and shoe boxes. There are plenty of creative, inexpensive, unexpected ways to contain your clutter *and* to disguise just how much of it you have. Here, simple solutions for dividing and conquering that will have you thinking outside the (cardboard) box.

Until science develops a self-organizing house, the best way to fight the chaos of clutter is through storage. There are two types of storage: short term and long term. Short-term storage is for items that you use frequently or daily, like underwear, silverware, or the kids' backpacks. Long-term storage is for things that you need only occasionally, such as thermal underwear, Grandma's punch ladle, and your pup tent. Your basement, garage, and attic (from the Latin, for "the place to hide out-of-season crap") are naturals for long-term storage. Outfit them with shelving and lots of lidded rubber containers filled with rarely used items. Use a label maker to identify the contents.

Short-term storage, for day-to-day essentials and things you need on a weekly basis, should be incorporated stylishly into your décor. All of it should be neatly corralled and organized for quick access. Unfortunately, this is the stage in the process where most folks lapse into disorderly conduct. They go for a bunch of small-scale solutions, like one CD tower and a single bookcase, both of which would visually chop up the room so that the space looks more, not less, cluttered. Better to go bold with a dramatic gesture. Remember, that's what high-impact is all about. Here, some suggestions you could use just about anywhere in your house, followed by those that are more room specific.

Here, there, anywhere

- Cover an entire wall with floor-to-ceiling shelves that can house both your music collection and your library in one central spot.
- Elevate a humble container by using it in multiples. Rows of metal beach pails, groupings of glass fishbowls, even a collection of large-size Chinese take-out cartons (unused, of course) all make for nifty nooks to stash your stuff in. Repetition adds impact!
- Take a cue from the Shaker style by installing peg rails down the length of a hall or around an entire room, then hang everything from Fido's leash, to clothes, to, well, extra chairs.
- Turn your stuff into utilitarian artwork. Line a hallway with two dozen (or so) small metal hooks, staggered at various heights, then hang handbags, hats, or colorful umbrellas.

In the family room

- Pressed-wood entertainment centers lack style and substance—they quickly look bedraggled, and fall apart not long thereafter. A more practical alternative? Clean-lined industrial steel shelving, a staple of restaurant kitchens that can hold hundreds of pounds, not to mention your entertainment system. They can be purchased directly from a restaurant supply company or home improvement store. For high impact, spray paint the shelves a bold, radioactive hue—high-visibility orange or nuke-blast yellow.

- CDs don't have to be stacked haphazardly in messy piles near the stereo—not when they can be transformed into eye candy. Slip the discs into CD "wallpaper," a poster-sized piece of vinyl with 24 CD-sized see-through pockets. For high impact, buy enough to cover an entire wall completely. (Check online stores specializing in storage.)

- Storage ottomans are multipurpose godsends that can hide everything from seasonal blankets to kids' toys. Group two or more of the square versions to form a coffee table. Think of the lids you'll be frequently lifting as an added incentive not to pile stuff on top.

- Quit feeling guilty that you haven't scrapbooked last year's vacation photos into your album. Just dump the snapshots into a decorative bowl and set them on the coffee table for everyone to sift

above and left: SHELF IMPROVEMENT: KEEP OPEN BOOKCASES LOOKING TIDY BY NEATLY—AND CREATIVELY—ARRANGING THE CONTENTS. THESE FLOOR-TO-CEILING CUBBYHOLES GO FROM WORKADAY TO WORK OF ART COURTESY OF DEEP WICKER BASKETS (WHICH HOUSE CLUTTER THAT'S BEST LEFT UNSEEN), STRATEGICALLY PLACED VASES, AND RUSTIC STACKS OF FIREWOOD.

through. Or buy a dozen archival photo boxes and affix large outdoor house numbers from the hardware store on the front. Line the boxes up in numerical order on your bookcase shelves, then every month stash the appropriate photos in the appropriate box.

- Buy a trio of five-foot-long unfinished wooden benches and paint them to complement the room's color scheme. Stack one atop the other to make a bookcase for magazines or videos.
- Turn file cabinets into side tables: top with a laminate-covered board or painted plywood, then skirt with fabric attached with Velcro.

In the kitchen

- No room for a pantry? On an unused wall, install shallow shelves that measure one canning jar deep. Line with canned goods or dozens of identical-sized glass jars filled with pasta, crackers, tea bags, you name it. If you want to hide your foodstuffs, conceal the shelves by hanging a floor-to-ceiling curtain in a sumptuous silk or velvet, or perhaps a more rustic-looking heavy linen. Mount the curtain on hospital tracks.
- Free up cupboard space by hanging your pots and pans from S-hooks attached to wall-mounted pegboard. Or, for an inexpensive overhead pot rack, buy a length of metal garden gate from a home improvement store and bolt it to the ceiling. Use S-hooks for utensils, too.
- Store spices in glass test tubes from a medical supply company, or use magnetic spice jars and stick directly onto the fridge.

In the bathroom

- Nothing spoils a spa feel like garish plastic packaging. Take sundries like cotton balls and Q-tips out of their packages and store them in metal-lidded glass canisters from a medical supply company. Transfer mouthwash and astringent to labeled glass decanters.
- Stash dirty towels in cheerful Mexican nylon mesh bags hung from hooks on the back of the bathroom door.
- Fill a gallon glass container with extra washcloths, bars of soap, rubber duckies, or bath puffs, and set it on the floor near the tub.
- Mount teak shelves or a metal étagère on the wall above the toilet tank.
- Roll bulky bath towels and stand them upright in a big wicker basket or large canvas tote bag (available at camping supply stores).
- If your sink doesn't include a vanity, skirt it with terry cloth attached with hook-and-loop tape. Put plastic shelving or a lazy Susan underneath and use to store extra rolls of toilet paper, cleaning supplies, and other essentials.

In the entryway

- Even if you don't have an entrance hall per se, there's always wall space for installing a shelf-and-hook combo to hold keys, a cell phone, and a stray jacket or two. Paint a 12-inch "frame" around the shelf in a contrasting color for graphic sass.
- A bench with cubbyholes underneath (holding baskets or buckets) provides a handy catch-all for school backpacks, sports equipment, and cold-weather accessories like mittens and scarves. Add bright cushions on top in sturdy fabrics.
- Use industrial-size cookie sheets from a restaurant supply store as drying racks for wet shoes.

PART II

OBJECTS TO INSPIRE

TRAVELING ACROSS the country gives me the opportunity to hear the design dilemmas facing DIY decorators and offer advice based on my own experiences. People often ask me: "How do you come up with your ideas?" "How do you get started?" "Why do you look so much better in person than you do on television?" (Please, people, just adjust your sets.)

I tell those inquiring minds that sometimes ideas come zooming at me like missiles I have to dodge. Sometimes, though, coming up with an idea can be a tedious process. In the fall of 1999 I participated in a prestigious charity event, the New York City Millennium Decorator Showhouse. I was given a small maid's room in which to work my magic. (This was my first actual "room"—previously I'd done entryways and hallways.) However, the creative spark was slow to catch fire. I would have settled for embers, but—zilch. I saw my career going up in flames. How did this happen? Maybe the pressure of Manhattan's hottest interior designers working right next door intimidated me, or this space was just a difficult one to maneuver. Who knows? The only thing I knew for certain was that barrenness was seriously out of character for me. The deadline was breathing down my neck, I was becoming more and more panicked, and I considered bailing out of the project—which might have derailed my design career before it even got on track. That is, until the night I walked (although "paced" is probably more accurate) past Ralph Lauren's flagship store on the Upper East Side. There, in the illuminated window, I spied an ottoman covered in zebra skin. It was exotic, sexy, sophisticated, reminiscent of the British Raj and an Ernest Hemingway safari—and I knew I had found my muse.

The room I eventually created for the Show House was a flat-out sensation. Using layers of crackling glaze and tints, I painted the walls to look like a brown-and-white zebra hide; a chenille-covered chaise longue, dhurry area rugs, and oversized mirrors all combined in a classic yet unexpected mix. The buzz from that zebra room led to ever-increasing press attention that eventually landed me on *Trading Spaces*. I'm guessing I owe Ralph some serious residuals by now.

The point of all this? Well, mostly that the whole creative process is simultaneously—and maddeningly—opaque and transparent. I don't know exactly why that ottoman embedded itself in my mind, but I do know that I can trace the genesis of an entire room back to it piece by piece. And it's the story I trot out whenever folks quiz me about the origin of my ideas. They see me concocting innovative room overhauls or outlandish artwork and want me to deconstruct my creative process. And while I hate to disappoint them, there isn't some big box store called Ideas-'R'-Us where you can load up on two-for-one idea specials. Creativity isn't a commodity you can buy—but it is an art you can learn, even if you think you're idea-challenged. Yes, you can actually train your brain to make those all-important *a-ha!* connections that are the basis of innovative interior design, which is what this chapter is all about. On the following pages, you'll trace how I brainstorm using an ordinary, everyday object—what I call a kick start—to create a fully decorated room.

WHERE DO IDEAS COME FROM?

Ideas don't occur in a vacuum. If your first stop in planning a design scheme for your room is the paint store, you're guaranteed to be overwhelmed by all the choices. Ditto choosing floor coverings, furniture, and accessories. Even having a general idea of the style you like best—say nouveau Moroccan or mid-century modern—will only help you narrow down your choices so far, and worse, can end up resulting in one of those predictable matchy-matchy rooms that say a lot about

a retailer's merchandising abilities and very little about your individual taste and style.

Every room I design starts with one inspirational item, the touchstone to which I return each time I introduce another element. I call these objects my kick start because they really get my creativity going. These idea sparkers can be anything, from the tangible to the intangible, an everyday object—or even a song that brings me back to a place and time. Whatever it may be that sends me on a creative journey, a design scheme can always be traced back to the first step. By using these kick starts as the starting point for your room, you can create a visual flowchart of your thought process.

Think about the things that make you happy. Is there an object you really, really love? It could be a piece of fabric you picked up on a vacation, a pattern on a piece of china from your grandmother's closet, or a sculptural item you bought on a whim. Maybe it's a favorite book or movie; or the ambiance of a restaurant you want for your dining room. As long as it's something that speaks to you, it's a kick start. Now begin to think about the characteristics of this kick start—is it brash or quiet, textured or smooth, angular or rounded, primary or pastel? As you answer these questions you're also making choices that will determine what else you'll introduce into the room.

On the following pages I'll walk you through the process with a few of the kick starts I've used recently to create fully realized design schemes, from window treatments to artwork to decorative finishing touches.

floor tile

fabric

vase

Vacation memories

Bring back more than just souvenirs from your travels—use the memory of a favorite vacation destination to create distinctive-looking décor. Here, a trip to the sun-soaked sandstone rock formations at Colorado Springs' Garden of the Gods influenced the choice of vibrant earth tones in a southwestern living room. Quarry tile in a scarlet shade mimics the park's geology and provides cool flooring during intense summer heat. The walls, color washed in three shades of orange that includes terra cotta, fruit punch, and agate, seem bathed in late-afternoon sunlight. Fabrics for pillows and curtains, which include a shimmery orange faux silk and a more formal yellow-and-red pattern, pull their energetic colors from the wall treatments. A solid, cowboy-brown leather sofa grounds all the orange shades, while kilim pillow covers in nubby wool add textural contrast. Soothing natural elements, like an arrangement of gerbera daisies in eye-popping yellow and a rustic vase constructed of windblown wood, look as if they were casually collected on a day-long mountain trek.

pillow cover

wall colors

sofa

fabric

accent tile

island

blinds

Silk leaf

The delicate lines and gossamer texture of this flirty craft store leaf, once used to decorate a birthday gift from one close friend to another and preserved as a memento, inspired the décor of an entire kitchen. A sumptuous silk fabric with an abstract fern motif has almost identical coloring, and is perfect for covering counter stools or banquette pillows. An accent tile with a leaf design continues the formal garden theme, as does the linen fabric for the curtains—all done in a fresh, summery green. For an airy outdoor feel, choose a light maple faux-wood floor and a kitchen island with crisp white cabinets; the decorative finial in a classic fleur-de-lis shape can be incorporated into the cabinetry for a touch of Old World elegance, or as a single accessory. Mixing it up are tortoiseshell wooden blinds, which add depth and texture and a bit of woodsy rusticity. And to keep things from getting too twee, liven up the place settings with cheerful Fiestaware in vibrant colors or muted shades depending on your taste.

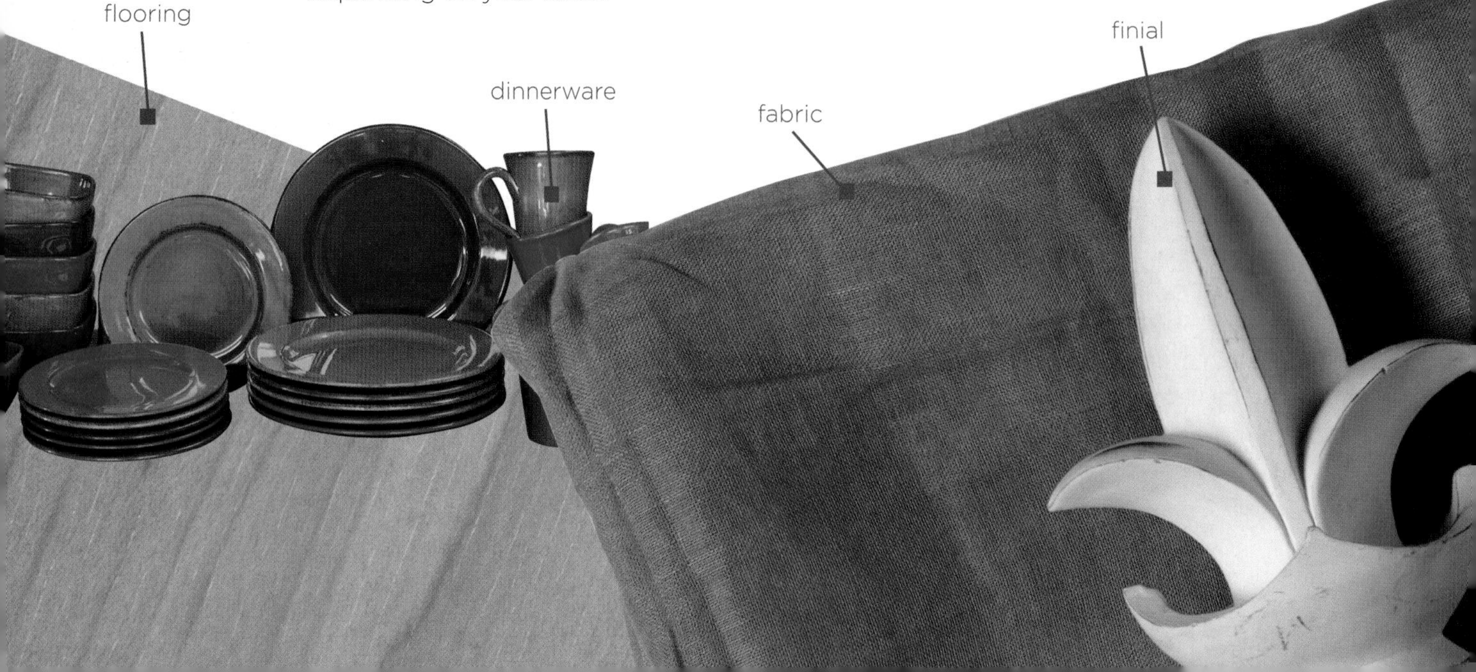

flooring

dinnerware

fabric

finial

floor

carpet

lighting

wall covering

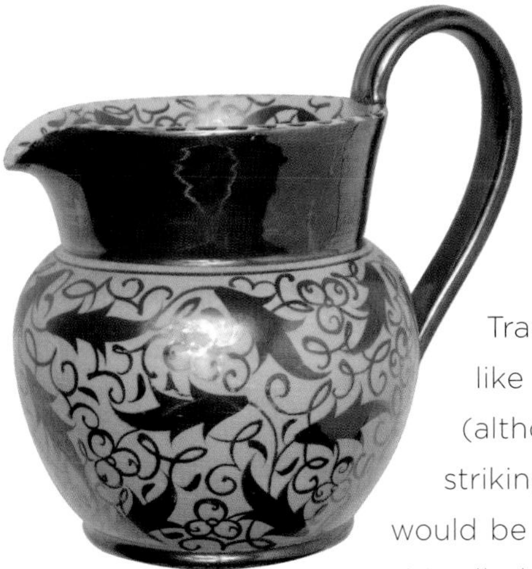

Pitcher

Traditional doesn't have to be boring. Looking like it was plucked from a Moroccan souk (although it's actually made by Wedgwood), this striking pitcher is a family heirloom. And while it would be perfectly at home in a classical setting, to me it's all about the exotic motif. To capitalize on that ethnic feel, I chose an opulent, Asian-ish curtain fabric embroidered with a leaf-and-bird pattern in rich shades of marigold, green, and blue. Balancing the luxe curtains and echoing the pitcher's metallic shimmer is sumptuous silvery gold tea-leaf wallpaper. Silky pillow covers in regal purple, ivory, and salmon, edged in delicate beading, continue the multicultural theme. Equally as dramatic: an iron-and-crystal chandelier with embellishments that resemble a mosque's minarets. Underfoot, a faux Persian wool carpet with a hand-knit fringe and muted colors doesn't compete with the curtain fabric, yet still stands out against a traditional, mahogany-stained floor.

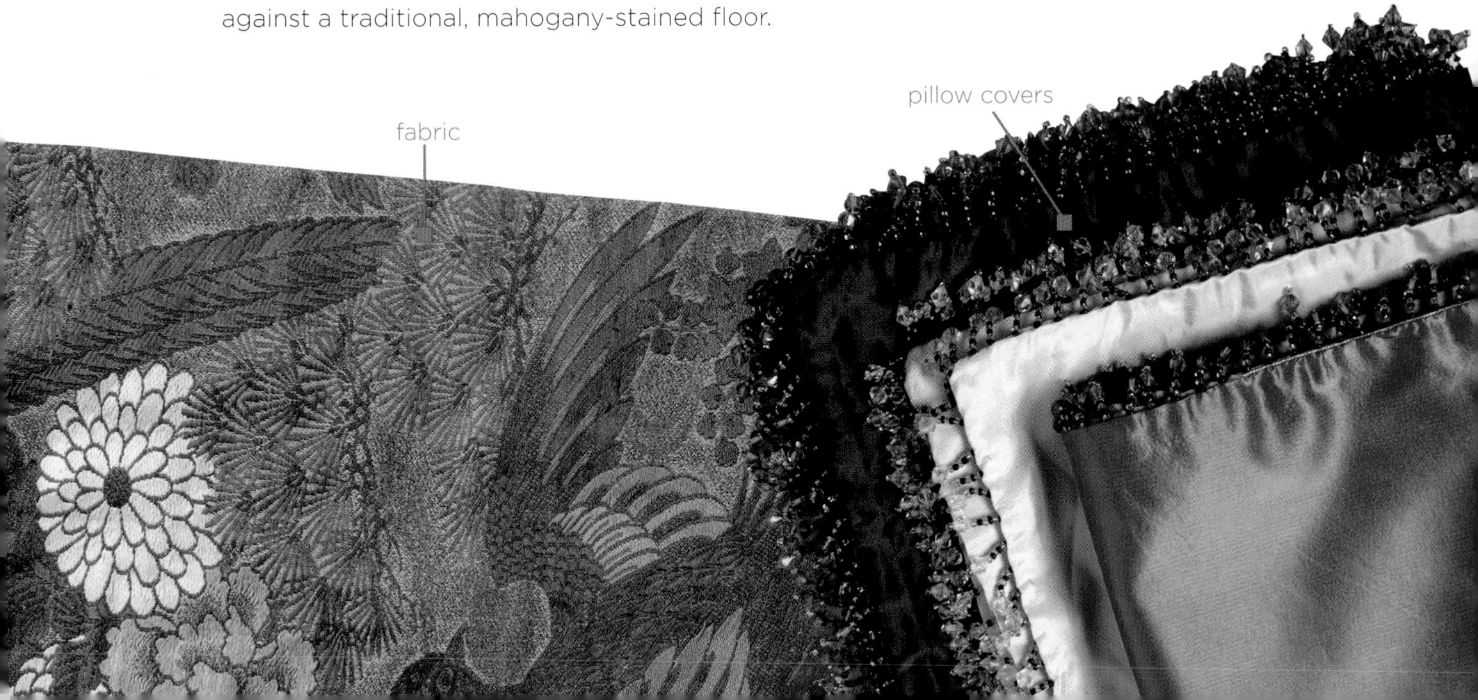

fabric

pillow covers

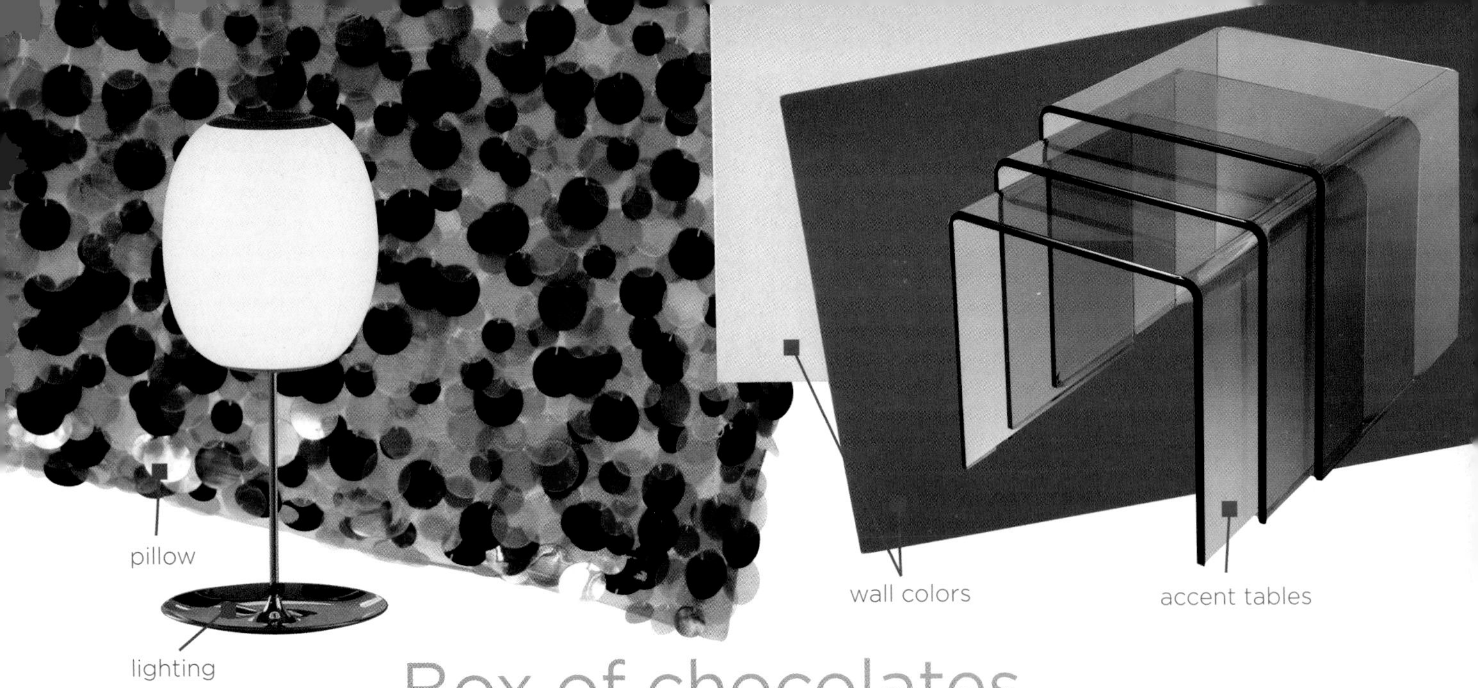

pillow

lighting

wall colors

accent tables

Box of chocolates

Commercial design and packaging can be a great source of inspiration. A dedicated chocoholic gave me this chic purple hatbox, which originally contained an addict's stash of high-end chocolates. It immediately made me think of a teenage girl's bedroom. An assortment of bedding and curtain fabrics—shimmery lilac satin, trippy purple linen, subtly sophisticated stripes, funky faux ivory leather—matches the hatbox's sassy color scheme, and a light lavender and purple wall paint ties the various shades together. Since the hatbox's mod shape is reminiscent of the swinging sixties, opt for furniture and accessories with a groovy bent: a purple throw pillow with psychedelic sequins, a table lamp as stylish as a pair of go-go boots, and nesting tables in futuristic plastic that can be fanned out when friends drop over to chill and "study." Of course, practicality is also a consideration. A low, linear bed made from white-lacquered wood veneer will fit into the room's retro theme—and any parent's budget.

fabric

fabric

bed

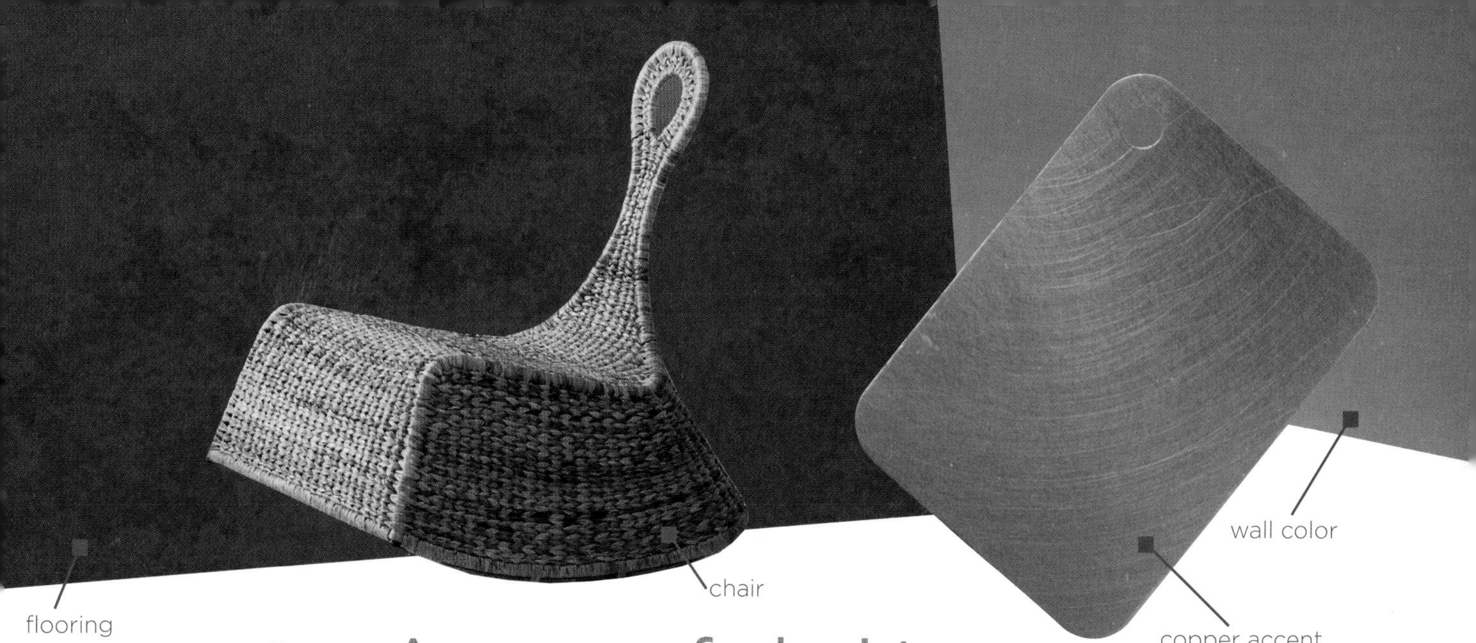

flooring

chair

wall color

copper accent

Aroma of chai tea

Not all kick starts have to be tangible, visual cues; smells can be incredibly evocative. A steaming cup of chai tea, spiced with sweet cinnamon, sharp ginger, and pungent clove, conjures up India's fertile Assam valley, with its hundreds of tea plantations on the banks of the Brahmaputra River. If that aroma were a living room pillow, it would be this fanciful tangerine number, delicately embroidered with green threads and studded with tiny mirrors. Pulling the paint color from the pillow yielded a soft shade of pine, which plays off the rough-textured seagrass rug. Shapely, low-to-the-ground rattan loungers also provide texture and capture the relaxed casualness of a coffeehouse. Cinnamon-colored copper, whether hammered onto an end table or molded into a wall sculpture, reinforces that sense of unwinding in a hip java joint filled with gleaming espresso makers. Smooth, gray slate flooring adds some unexpected contrast, while a lidded, acorn-topped wood cachepot is a handy spot for storing loose tea.

pillow

rug

fabric

lighting

wall color

Striped handbag

How can a living room resemble a handbag? When you translate the pocketbook's quirky combo of youthful and sophisticated notes—saucy stripes plus a classic shape—into a décor that's part modern and part traditional (much like its owner). Here, the purse's proper brown leather trim translates into a practical chocolate carpet, while the bag's rakish lavender-purple stripe yielded the fresh-looking wall color. A matching chair and ottoman in ivory microsuede, plus an overhead fixture with a repeating pattern of glass squares, captures the bag's clean lines. A mottled cashmere yarn, for creating open stitching on a pillow, keeps the look nicely off-kilter by bringing some handmade coziness to all the modernity. Shiny fabrics in light crimson, pumpkin, and golden saffron brighten and exaggerate the colors in the yarn, and add some zest to the room when they're sewn into curtains.

chair and ottoman

carpet

pillow accent

tile accent

wall sample

sofa

fabric

Woman's scarf

Your home can feel as familiar and comfy as a favorite pair of broken-in jeans if you look to your wardrobe for decorating cues. That was the case with this three-toned green scarf, purchased from a street vendor. Its versatile hues sparked the look for two styles of living rooms—one traditional, the other modern—after I discovered curtain panels in scarf-matching shades of moss, sage, and olive. Three possible wall treatments—a jazzy glaze finish, a classic muted wash, or high-gloss venetian plaster that could swing both ways—all have a subtle green tinge to complement the window treatments, while a mosaic accent tile composed of variegated green squares helps to punch up the seafoam palette. A trio of additional fabrics for slipcovers and pillows includes a silky stripe, an exotic faux silk with gold beading, and a linen-and-silk combo with an almost grainy texture. A dark-wood armoire with crown molding and an overstuffed sofa in either ivory or dark sage work in almost any kind of design setting; the room's topped off with a style-spanning pewter chandelier with flame-shaped bulbs.

wall sample

armoire

wall sample

sofa

fabric

lighting

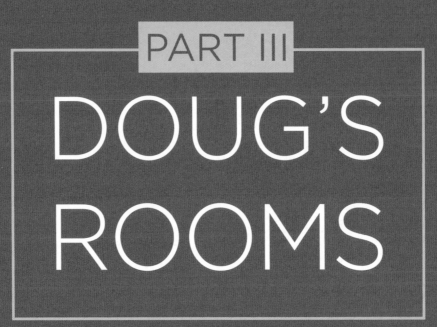

PART III

DOUG'S ROOMS

HE PASSION FOR GARDENING

INVITATION TO THE
GARDEN

RIGHT NOW, I feel exactly the way I did at age 15 on the opening night of *Annie Get Your Gun.* It was my first time on stage as a professional in a full-fledged acting role, and I was both panicked and exhilarated. This was dinner theater in rural Illinois, and for a teenage thespian with dreams of stardom, it was the big time, baby. For days, I had memorized lines, rehearsed dance steps, learned how to handle my props, even helped install the set and hang the lights. Sure, I had done all the advance prep work, but would I be able to perform under pressure? And could I be heard over the sounds of all that clinking glassware? Believe me: until a live audience is seated out front and the curtain goes up, you just don't know if you'll fall flat or break a leg.

Thank god, my legs were intact and I could hold my head high during the finale. I hope that after you check out this chapter, which brings together in convenient room form all the decorating principles and practical techniques I've just detailed, you'll agree that I've done it again. You'll see the specific sources of inspiration that kicked off the creative process, and the unexpected ways I combined the five basic rules of high-impact design—proportion and scale, furniture placement, color, lighting, and clutter management—to create surprising, and occasionally irreverent, spaces. These aren't bland, seen-'em-before interiors, and you probably won't want to duplicate everything shown here in your own home—which is exactly the point. Cookie-cutter sameness (even if it is high-impact) is boring, so feel free to improvise and improve upon my designs and interpret them in a palette and style more in keeping with *your* taste.

Okay, it's time to flip the page and see what you think of the production. Just remember that once you're done, you'll have all the necessary tools to be your own decorator—and it'll be your turn in the spotlight. (And if you happen to land an agent who takes less than 10 percent, give me a call.)

CHEEKY TIKI

Trading Spaces fans always want me to name my most difficult room redo, assuming I'll launch into a crazed, acid-tongued diatribe about stripping flocked velvet wallpaper and browbeating homeowners suffering from sleep deprivation. I wish. My biggest challenge was actually this 18-by-14-foot media room. The location? My own offices. (I'm a demanding client, what can I say?) The headquarters of my design business, which occupies the entire third floor of a nineteenth-century brownstone on Manhattan's Upper East Side, this room needed to be a major multitasker. It had to

kick start

I spotted this offbeat cookie jar (which I promptly dubbed Tiki Guy) at a home décor store where it was languishing in the clearance rack—probably because most people thought it looked like surplus from a defunct Polynesian restaurant. Which is exactly why I bought it. The quirky sienna color and Trader Vic retro vibe (flaming pupu platter, anyone?) influenced the entire room—from the circa-1970s tangerine-and-chocolate palette to the rustic wicker baskets and tortoiseshell blinds. Not bad for a $20 piece of passed-over pottery.

TURN TO PAGE 170 TO LEARN HOW TO "ANTIQUE" WICKER BASKETS.

be a quiet personal workspace where I could run my company, Douglas Wilson Ltd., plus an inviting spot for entertaining prospective clients. And since my own New York City pad is so tiny (if less is more, it has everything), it also had to be a home-away-from-home where I could host get-togethers with friends.

Since I wasn't constrained by anyone but myself when it came to the décor, I really let loose with my signature style: a pared-down, classic, yet slightly irreverent scheme combined with a totally fearless approach to color. The bold tangerine walls instantly spark a "wow" reaction from first-time visitors, and though the look is rich and dimensional, it cost next to nothing to create. I just glued ordinary tissue paper right onto the walls. The shade feels sophisticated, not cartoonish, because I added chocolate accents to create a timeless, brown-and-orange color combination that's slightly 1970s, but in a good, nonpolyester kind of way.

To emphasize the height of the 11-foot ceilings, I opted for a low-to-the-ground sectional sofa that's long enough for lounging and napping (hey, it's not like it's IBM corporate here). I also employed another visual trick to draw the eye upward: vertically stacking inexpensive Ikea bookcases. Painting all these shelving units the same shade of cocoa brown made them look like expensive built-ins and created an eye-pleasing contrast against the orange walls.

Multiple coats of paint applied by previous renters had left the walls as bumpy as cellulite—and about as appealing. But the expense and bother of smoothing out all those dimpled and lumpy layers, replastering, and then painting was something I didn't want to undertake in a rental space that I planned to occupy for only a short time.

So I disguised the uneven, unattractive walls by randomly gluing on rectangles and squares of inexpensive craft store tissue paper, overlapping them to create shades of varying intensity. The whole wall is sealed with polyurethane and tinted with glaze to create a slightly aged effect. Even if

do-it-yourself projects usually drive you up a wall, this is a cheap, simple technique that can hide less-than-perfect walls.

Of course, walls this dramatic need to be paired with more subdued furniture. The L-shaped sofa, in an understated shade of taupe, is surprisingly versatile—with its contemporary lines and brushed-aluminum legs, the mid-century design can blend with a variety of décors.

The overall effect of this unconventional office? Inviting, warm, and cozy—in other words, a room that reflects the real me. Honest.

TURN TO PAGE 164 TO LEARN HOW TO TISSUE-PAPER A WALL.

fast fix

Whoopee, cushions! Tossing some flamboyant throw pillows into your décor is the easiest way to reenergize a stagnant-looking room—and hide stubborn upholstery stains. Here, autumnal-hued toss pillows in a variety of fabrics, including chenille and silk (sewn from a vintage Christian Dior scarf), give the office a fall feel and echo the tangerine walls; when the weather turns warmer, I'll switch to lighter linen covers in shocking Pepto-Bismol pink—what, you think I'd choose some Pepto-Dismal color like ecru?

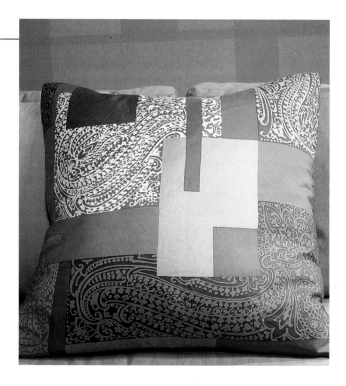

art of the matter

These oversized, minimalist canvases offer a restful spot for the eyes, like a visual vacation. The bold curves of paint contrast with the room's sharp-angled furniture, yet still mesh with the clean-lined décor.

TURN TO PAGE **168** TO LEARN HOW TO MAKE A FABRIC-COVERED FOLDING SCREEN.

APPLYING THE PRINCIPLES

PROPORTION AND SCALE

Selecting the correct-sized coffee table confuses a whole lot of people. As a general rule, coffee tables should be one-half to two-thirds the length of your sofa. Here, I chose an oversized, brass-topped steel coffee table with substantial dimensions—check out how a good chunk of it extends past the sofa—but it works for the space and my needs. The

sprawling surface can accommodate stacks of design magazines, take-out lunches, and piles of fabric swatches (usually all at the same time).

MANAGING CLUTTER

Sometimes, no amount of bins, boxes, or catch-alls can impose order on unsightly clutter. When that's the case, enlist a folding screen to keep your stuff out of sight but still easily accessible. Stretching almost to the ceiling, a hinged room divider completely walls off a full-size copier, fax, and printer in a corner of my office. To get the maximum impact from your screen savior, opt for dividers with panels in dramatic designs (different fabrics on each side of the screen allow you to switch it up when you need a change) or strong textures, like braided rope, birch twigs, or palm bark.

TURN TO PAGE 166 TO LEARN HOW TO MAKE A NO-SEW WINDOW VALANCE.

color commentary

Orange can sometimes be tricky on walls. This tangerine tissue paper looked way too bright when it was originally applied and utterly lacked that cozy, let's-linger hue I was hoping for. Stippling on a tinted glaze toned down the vibrancy, deepening the orange almost to a burnt red where the tissue squares overlapped.

Keep in mind that a brown ceiling like this is tough to pull off in rooms with standard 8- or 9-foot ceiling heights because the dark color makes the space feel smaller. The cocoa works here because the room's one standout feature is the gracious, 11-foot ceiling. Besides, a more traditional off-white ceiling color would have looked stark next to the tangerine walls, leaving the room feeling cold, not comfy.

FRENCH TWIST

Call me strange, but I've always had a thing for tornadoes. While I was growing up, the folks in my rural farming community were terrified of them and rightly so, but I always viewed twisters as a rare source of entertainment. (C'mon, it was the sticks, there wasn't a lot of excitement.) Of course, now that I live at a safe remove from this meteorological mayhem, funnel clouds are a source of nostalgia—and decorating inspiration. Although I never got the chance to install a wind machine and unleash a tornado-themed room on *Trading Spaces* (for which Paige and her hairdresser

kick start

What happens when you cross poultry from the Illinois State Fair with Coco Chanel? You get the unlikely inspiration for this tongue-in-chic living room plus some dazzling-looking chickens. Granted, combining the influences of a legendary French fashion designer with barnyard animals might seem far-fetched, but nearly every summer as a kid I came face-to-beak with prizewinning ornamental breeds of chickens whose plumage rivaled anything the famed couturier could dream up. You should have seen their feathered finery laced with narrow edgings of black, frizzled into delicate poufs, cascading in elegantly unkempt tresses.

The memories of those exotic pullets and bantams rushed back to me on a recent Parisian vacation, when I saw firsthand the outrageous embellishments and artistry of the garments at the Chanel boutique. These over-the-top outfits looked awfully similar to the flamboyant feathers of the state-fair chickens (except larger, and made for people). That's when I realized the distance between an exclusive, first arrondissement shop in the City of Light wasn't that far from a chicken coop in Illinois—and hit upon a perfect pairing for an American living room in need of to-the-hilt glamour.

TURN TO PAGE **171** TO LEARN HOW TO COVER A DRESSER IN FABRIC.

are eternally grateful), I was finally able to indulge my appreciation for all things cyclone in this suburban living room.

The fashion-forward owner, who has a weakness for couture pink, wanted a space that was elegant and flirty without being traditional. A coal color on the walls was the easiest, cheapest way to inject catwalk-worthy drama into the space. The high-impact black was a daring decorating choice, but the overall effect is modern, not macabre, thanks to the room's plentiful natural light and playful touches: flocks of ceramic chickens and cotton-candy-pink accessories. *Noir* walls also provide a seamless backdrop for elegant but eclectic furniture, like an Ikea dresser outfitted in a natty menswear tweed. For color contrast, I added a sumptuous white flokati (a Greek-made, fluffy wool rug), which offers the decadence of fur at a fraction of the price.

Investing in top quality furniture, such as an iconic Le Corbusier black leather armchair, makes good economic sense. Well-made pieces will hold up for decades, both stylistically and structurally. Of course, the main drawback with purchasing high-ticket items is that they're expensive, which means there's no surplus *dinero* for accessories and occasional furniture. The solution: Witty, wallet-friendly fill-ins that rely more on creativity than cash for their appeal. Like these ceramic barnyard biddies I discovered at a craft store, which convincingly mimic antique porcelain for not much more than chicken feed—talk about cheep! I arranged them playfully on the coffee table, but they can also be perched atop wall-hung plaster brackets.

Maybe this calamine-pink and black room—sort of traditional, with a twist (or make that, a twister)—is too unsettling for you. Well, you can always close your eyes, click your (Jimmy Choo) heels together, and repeat, "There's no place like *my* home, there's no place like *my* home."

fast fix

Wake up and smell the Starbucks, people: You can use furniture any way you damn well please, regardless of its intended purpose. Like these inexpensive end tables from Ikea, which I configured into a sly, black-and-white coffee table. Repurposing items like this shows off your creativity and turns the tables on the tyranny of high-priced furniture.

APPLYING THE PRINCIPLES

PROPORTION AND SCALE

Oversized photographs prevent the prominent picture window from overpowering the space. Seating was kept purposefully low to counter the window's pronounced verticality (that's decorator speak for, "it's wide *and* tall").

FURNITURE PLACEMENT

Rooms without a natural focal point, like a fireplace or—ahem—a television, sometimes require trial-and-error decorating and rejiggering. I originally had this couch floating in the middle of the room, facing a chair and the picture window with its sweeping backyard view. But the seven-foot-long couch was so immense it was off-putting, as if it was (literally) turning its back on visitors; the chair also seemed too insubstantial next to the oversized windows. Switching the sofa to its current spot created a friendlier, more welcoming feel, while still offering plenty of outdoor-gazing entertainment. A flokati rug forms a conversational area around the sofa and a logical boundary for positioning the furniture.

color commentary

Jet black walls aren't for the timid, or for those decorating a nursery—unless you're raising Rosemary's baby. But if you're daring enough to look past the dungeon connotations, you'll discover that black walls, like the proverbial little black dress, can impart instant sophistication. Pink also transforms when paired with black. Often it's too confectionary for anything but a little girl's bedroom, but here it's cosmopolitan and sassy. In another setting, inexpensive tables and ceramic chickens could have seemed trashy, not classy.

Of course, black magic requires some sleight of hand. Black paint will reveal every flaw in a wall, so make sure to smooth out the surface beforehand, prime with a dark primer, and sand between every coat—*including* the primer—with fine-grit sandpaper. Because it's a noncolor that absorbs light, black can seem flat, so I compensated by adding lots of texture to the room: faux leather throw pillows, a fluffy area rug, billowy linen curtains, and a dresser swaddled in a couture-inspired tweed fabric.

Avoid black walls if you have fussy furnishings like paisley sofas and Victorian horsehair chairs. This severe shade looks best with sleek pieces and neutral upholstery in crisp shades of gray, ivory, tan, and khaki.

art of the matter

It may look like high-end art photography, but this pair of cyclone prints started out as nondescript 8-by-10 color photographs that I purchased online. My neighborhood copy shop converted the images to black and white, heightened the contrast, then enlarged them to poster proportions—for hundreds of dollars less than similar-sized photographs would have cost at a gallery. Hung in minimalist frames, the prints are as chic as they are inexpensive.

CENTRAL BARK

How did the dining room get so uptight? There it is, right off the kitchen, arguably the friendliest room in the house, yet it sees action only twice a year. Blame this neglect on the typical dining room's formality: the matching furniture suite, the crystal chandeliers, all that breakable glassware—exactly what the owner of this urban dining room didn't want. Instead, she was after an easy elegance that wasn't intimidating or off-putting. Simple and minimal, this dining space is all about livability and style on a budget, with easy-care furniture and fabrics that are anything but fussy.

TURN TO PAGE 174 TO LEARN
HOW TO STENCIL A CURTAIN.

kick start

The owner's foliage photos were a rich source of inspiration. Taken with a telephoto lens, the images reveal an intimate aspect of plants most of us don't take the time to see: the intricate veining, the perfectly symmetrical edging, the deep and varied shadings of green. Enlarged by an imaging shop and mounted on 2-foot-by-3-foot gator board (a sturdier, longer-lasting version of Foamcore), the leaves changed from realistic, to abstract, to works of art.

It was a nearby park that provided the decorating cues and the earthy color palette for this room. The homeowner, an avid amateur photographer, had shot extreme close-ups of plants during a nature walk. The resulting pictures were so green and graphically interesting, I made them the focal point of the room by enlarging them to poster size and hanging a trio on the longest wall.

Since the client lacked the desire—and the big bucks—for upholstered dining chairs or a traditional Oriental rug, I injected softness and texture into the space with fabric. Lavish-looking drapes that puddle extravagantly on the floor were sewn from plain, $2-a-yard burlap. This utilitarian fabric, a gardening mainstay that's used for wrapping root balls and protecting shrubbery, has a coarse weave and woodsy color that's in keeping with the room's

fast fix

Like a roaring fire but don't have a backyard for your wood pile? You could stash all those extra logs in a cupboard or closet, but it's a space waster—not to mention messy to access. A better solution: turn the kindling into an artful arrangement. Here, neatly stacked firewood placed strategically between the two windows creates an earthy, rugged sculpture.

straightforward aesthetic. For a touch of simple elegance and graphic interest, a repeating fern pattern was stenciled onto the curtains in the same white color as the walls.

Furnishing a dining room on a budget can leave a bad taste in your mouth. Formal suites that include matching chairs, table, and sideboard usually cost a fortune, while lower-priced versions often look better suited for a kitchen.

So I kept furniture costs low by purchasing the dining table at what just may be the least likely place imaginable: a used office furniture emporium. Among the filing cabinets and office chairs, I found a round laminate conference table perfectly proportioned for the dining space. A round table works best for dinner parties—conversation flows much easier when all the guests can see one another—and the slightly damaged surface and support post weren't deal breakers. I just covered the entire thing with a sumptuous green tablecloth in a faux silk that billows all the way to the floor, and no one is the wiser about what's lurking underneath. A quartet of square-backed rattan chairs from an import store add sophistication without stuffiness and are surprisingly comfortable.

color commentary

To me, white walls are the decorative equivalent of white noise: they're so unexciting and uninspired they just fade into the background. But sometimes that can actually be a positive (or a necessity—some leases stipulate white walls only), which was the case here. The leaf photographs were such a dazzling green, they needed something plain and unobtrusive to really showcase them, like the white walls of a museum. Of course, I didn't just slap up some random shade of white. I chose an off-white ivory that's bright without being blinding, never looks dingy, and has bone undertones.

TURN TO PAGE **176** TO LEARN
HOW TO PAPER A CEILING IN TREE BARK.

APPLYING THE PRINCIPLES

PROPORTION AND SCALE

Since dining rooms are the least multipurpose spaces in a house, why not just emphasize that fact—with the biggest dining table
you can fit through the doorway? A jumbo,
globe-shaped paper lantern lessens the
visual dominance of the table and plays it up
at the same time.

FURNITURE PLACEMENT

To take the emphasis off the nonworking fireplace, I positioned the table smack in the
middle of the room. A narrow console table
nearby allows for easy movement around the
dining chairs, and also balances the shape
and height of the fireplace surround.

LIGHTING

In a dining room this unfussy, an opulent
chandelier dangling with bobeches and glass
teardrops would look out of place. A Noguchi-
style paper lantern from an import store lights
up the room for less than $30, and provides
ample illumination for the diners below. Talk
about sitting pretty.

ASIAN FUSION

When you're raised in a small rural town, the Chinese restaurant 30 miles away passes for exotic. The fact that I never actually ate there (my father's unwavering Midwestern palate leaned more toward meat-and-potato menus) only increased its mysterious allure. Now, I'm an Asian food addict—Hildi and I are always hunting down sushi bars whenever we're on a *Trading Spaces* assignment. (And to set the record straight: I did *not* lose the wasabi-eating contest. She cheated.)

color commentary

For this over-the-top red color scheme, I took design cues from imperial Beijing and from *manga,* Japanese comic books known for their intensely saturated hues. Painting the walls in an oh-my-god crimson shade as bold as a geisha's lipstick made the room feel sociable, inviting, and sultry.

TURN TO PAGE 180 TO LEARN HOW TO PAINT A CHINOISERIE MURAL.

Eastern decor still has a transporting effect on me, although its austerity can be tough to live with long-term—just ask anyone with a toddler and a paper shoji screen mended with duct tape.

That's why for this supersized family room, I created a user-friendly Asian design that's warm and welcoming, yet still visually arresting. It was a tall order because the space is so massive. This bigger-is-better phenomenon is something I frequently encounter when I'm taping *Trading Spaces*, especially in newly built developments. Often the rooms are so gargantuan that you need a trail of bread crumbs just to find your way out. While it's impressive to have cathedral ceilings or rooms in different zip codes under the same roof, it can be tough to bring all that largeness down to human scale—ever seen a cozy airplane hangar? Or the bill for decorating one?

To pull the space together and add intimacy, I laid a white shearling carpet that stretched nearly wall-to-wall. Yes, fur this size is a serious budget buster, but it feels as soft as cashmere underfoot and could double as extra seating if you're having a *Barbarella* moment. (You can also get the same effect via fake shearling, without the PETA protestors on your front lawn.) Fiery, Imperial Beijing red on the walls punches up the contrast with the white flooring and creates a toasty feel. A do-it-yourself chinoiserie mural that winds around the entire

kick start

For this family room's inspiration I turned to *Trading Spaces*'s second season, when I revamped a North Carolina bedroom with a chinoiserie mural. "China Blue," as I dubbed that extremely popular makeover (read: the homeowners didn't cry), featured similar drawings of pagodas, cranes, and bamboo. I had found the eighteenth-century mural sketch in an art book, and immediately fell in love with the understated motifs. The resulting mural, painted in soft white over vivid red, is as sophisticated as toile wallpaper, but a heck of a lot cheaper.

room also unifies the space, and substitutes for costly artwork.

Themed rooms can be the downfall of even the most well-intentioned designer. Go overboard with painstaking historical details or kitschy embellishments, and it's as if you're living inside a diorama. Asian rooms are particularly susceptible to orient excess, so I put my (bound) foot down: no clichéd paper fans, calligraphy scrolls, or Ho Chi miniatures. High-impact subtlety was my motto.

In fact, none of the furniture here is strictly Asian—it's actually a lot closer to modern than to Oriental reproductions, and it's all from Ikea—but it reads as multicultural because of the strong shapes. The pair of kid-size rattan loungers resemble the sinuous couches of a 1920s opium den. A low-to-the-ground coffee table could hold its own at a Japanese tea ceremony.

A mammoth room with no natural focal point can dissolve into visual chaos—unless you add something as off-the-charts zany as an outdoor swing. Aside from being one of my classic smart aleck touches—or, in designer-speak, an expression of my pronounced penchant for unorthodox pairings —it's a triple happiness: it was cheaper than an upholstered couch, had graceful lines that didn't obscure the murals, and literally gave the room movement and energy. How's that for being one smart (fortune) cookie?

APPLYING THE PRINCIPLES

MANAGING CLUTTER

Who says sideboards are only for dining rooms? These versatile pieces, with their long, lean lines and ample storage, are an open-and-shut case in clutter-clogged areas like family rooms. Try storing a television or stereo inside—or really raise the bar on style and repurpose a chic sideboard into a swinging cocktail bar, like I did with this sleek Ikea number. Essential mixology equipment such as swanky martini glasses and jiggers can be assembled on stainless steel trays (top the sideboard with a piece of glass if you're worried about spills); underneath, liquor and extra glassware are stowed neatly out of sight.

FURNITURE PLACEMENT

The sideboard's matching lamps create a symmetrical arrangement that's ultra traditional (flanking the sideboard with identical straight-back chairs would have the same effect, plus offer seating for unsteady tipplers). And I centered the rococo mirror—which actually *is* a nineteenth-century French antique that already belonged to the clients—precisely above the sideboard, old-school-style. Sure, suddenly going formal might raise a few eyebrows, but it will definitely lift your spirits.

TURN TO PAGE 178 TO LEARN HOW TO "LACQUER" A LAMP.

fast fix

Don't pass up the perfect lamp just because the color is wrong or the shade isn't right. This wooden number blends seamlessly with the room's Oriental décor—check out how the shape mimics the crenellated rooflines of a pagoda. Who would know that it started out a pale peach color with a foam-green, shirred shade? I just applied a few coats of paint with an aerosol sprayer for a lacquered look, then added a new square shade for an Asian de-light.

TURN TO PAGE 179 TO LEARN HOW TO PAINT A STRIPED LAMP SHADE.

POSH PUCCI

Living in a Manhattan high-rise is a lot like flying. You have a bird's-eye view of the cityscape below, you're surrounded by blue sky—and your accommodations usually have some of the same cramped dimensions as an airplane cabin. That doesn't have to be a bad thing. In this long, narrow, one-bedroom apartment, perched atop the fifteenth floor of a doorman building on the island's far west side, I slyly evoked the swinging sixties era of aviation's coffee-tea-or-me heyday. The owner, who works in television and throws a mean cocktail party, wanted a sexy, chic pad to showcase

her dramatic views of the Hudson River. The result, with plenty of built-in storage and space for entertaining, is anything but economy class.

The biggest problem in this space was, well, the space. The rooms lacked natural focal points like fireplaces; the windows weren't symmetrical; there were odd angles that jutted out from nowhere; and there wasn't a great flow from room to room.

For an apartment with this type of awkward layout and space limitations, dual-purpose built-ins are a necessity. The tiny dining alcove (annexed from part of the living room), was outfitted with a sleek white banquette instead of a set of space-gobbling dining chairs. The deep, custom-made seating conceals cupboards for hiding bulky kitchen items, and storage cabinets behind the banquette extend around the corner into a hallway, where they morph into a combination desk/bar. But form isn't sacrificed to function: the banquette is a stylish conversation pit during parties and fits right in with the living room's sophisticated pieces. Overhead, open glass shelves hold wine and mixers, and narrow cabinets conceal books and CDs. A funky, amethyst Lucite chair offers loads more sass than the typical black office chair.

Other solutions for deemphasizing the haphazard layout? Maintaining a hazy jet-blue color palette throughout the apartment, with the rooms painted in subtle variations of azure and blue-violet, and

laying identical pebbled tile flooring in both the kitchen and the bathroom, to tie together opposite ends of the maze. This combo of cool color and sleek surfaces was urban and edgy, but it also had the potential to be too chilly and stark. To soften the look, I added texture with unexpected accessories and furniture, like a furry cowhide area rug. Its dramatic black-and-white spotting and down-home charm play off the high-tech plasma television and built-ins, and give a knowing wink to the creamy leather side chair. A retro glass-and-chrome coffee table (made from a 1970s table base found at a flea market) is groovy without being too far out. Pulling it all together: a straightforward sofa in a sturdy wool flannel that's tailor-made for lounging.

└─color commentary

It's no surprise that most people say blue is their favorite hue. It's calming and soothing, the color of the sky and the ocean. That enveloping sense of serenity was exactly what this owner wanted, so I bathed the whole apartment in tones of azure and violet. In the kitchen and living room, with its oversize windows and doorway to the terrace, a dusty blue darkens to indigo after hours. For the bedroom, a tranquil lavender is an antidote to the city's stresses.

Bathrooms the size of a 747's lavatory are the norm in New York City, and this apartment's was no exception. Tiny, with bland fixtures and milk-colored tiles, it lacked the spa feel the current owner was after. Since the square footage and layout couldn't be altered, I added luxe upgrades instead, like a soaking tub and a raised-bowl marble sink and Dornbracht fixtures. Blue-violet tiles that complement the apartment's overall color scheme were mounted vertically to make the ceilings seem higher. Extending them beyond the shower stall to the vanity backsplash and up the walls created an

unbroken line that visually expands the space. I used the same technique with the organic-chic floor tiles from Artistic Tile—which have pebbles suspended in clear resin and create the illusion that you're viewing stones underwater—by running them all the way to the lip of the tub. A simple transparent shower curtain is in keeping with the minimalist mode and doesn't box in the tub with unnecessary color.

APPLYING THE PRINCIPLES

MANAGING CLUTTER

Acres of crisp, white built-ins keep the living room and dining areas looking minimalist, and conceal items best left behind closed doors.

PROPORTION AND SCALE/FURNITURE PLACEMENT

In the living room, sleek furniture doesn't compete with the vertical windows and stunning views; mounting a television on the sliver of wall between the balcony door and the picture window also helps keep the focus on that side of the room. The strongly angular sofa and side chair balance the visual weight of the dining room's banquette and the storage cabinets, with no jarringly oversize pieces to break all the long, continuous lines.

In such a contemporary apartment, I wasn't about to trick out the bedroom in a four-poster bed with frilly shams and a flouncy bed skirt. Yet I still wanted this space to feel like a sanctuary from the city that never sleeps. The solution: a dreamy, chic boutique hotel look, complete with a soothing palette and understated furnishings, that doesn't cost much more than a long weekend at one of Manhattan's tonier accommodations. Essential for creating the feel of an A-lister suite was the dra-

TURN TO PAGE 188 TO LEARN HOW
TO MAKE A PADDED HEADBOARD.

matic padded headboard. Constructed on the
cheap using plywood, batting, and ultrasuede, then
trimmed with mahogany-stained wood, the final
cost had the owner resting easy. Sheets and lamp
bases edged in tobacco brown repeat the outlining
motif for a restful, cohesive feel. The price for the

Matteo cotton sateen coverlet was eye-opening,
but since the periwinkle shade matched the wall
color, it wasn't worth losing sleep over.

If the kitchen is the heart of the home, this now-
elegant galley was originally on life support. Before
renovation, the faux-maple cabinets and outdated
linoleum were lackluster, and seemed even more
jarring next to the white appliances. Milky blue isn't

Standard cabinets are normally hung with a gap between the top of the cabinet and the ceiling because it's a quick and easy installation. That means the no man's land area above the cabinets becomes a dust collector, or a catchall for other "collectibles" like wicker baskets (three words: no, noo, nooo). You can get a cleaner, leaner look by replacing the standard doors with custom versions like the ones shown here. Taller than the actual cabinets, they provide extra storage that can be hidden away with the simple close of a door.

a typical kitchen color, but painting the walls, ceiling, and backsplash the same shade as the rest of the apartment immediately softened the look of the cramped quarters and blurred the line between where the cooking area ended and the nearby living room started. The owner didn't have a pot of money, so the existing cabinets were refaced, using fronts identical to the built-ins behind the dining banquette—yet another fool-the-eye trick to expand the dimensions of the apartment. The only advantage to a kitchen this pint-sized? Not having to spend a lot of dough on expanses of Corian countertops or pebble-and-resin tile. Only a few square feet of each was required, which made staying within the budget a piece of cake.

HEAVY PETAL

It wasn't some traumatic FTD incident or fisticuffs with Laura Ashley that triggered my aversion to floral décor. In fact, I don't harbor any dislike for flowers as long as they stay where they belong: in the garden or in a vase. (Yeah, yeah, I'm no shrinking violet when it comes to my views on flowers.) So it was a shocker when the owner of this vast sitting room mentioned that she wanted something . . . cottage-y. And pretty. In short, floral. Luckily, she allowed me to redefine English country cottage style, à la Doug Wilson. And the results, I must admit, are growing on me.

gardening PAUL THOMPSON

garden design MARGARET CROWTHER & SUE HOOK

KEN DRUSE THE PASSION FOR GARDENING

Martin Gardens of the Heartland

ROSES

The TULIP

color commentary

Combining lime-fizz walls with a blue-matted print and neon pink pillows might seem bizarre —until you take a closer look at the color combinations in a flowering garden. Mother Nature deftly mixes hundreds of hues that most of us would normally dismiss as incompatible. The next time you're hesitant about pairing seemingly disparate shades, leaf through a garden magazine or check out your local botanical garden for inspiration.

kickstart

This cheerful cotton fabric delivered the goods: the large-scale blooms are brash and abstract, and the colors are flower-child trippy. Still, I used the fabric in moderation, restricting it to the sheers and a scattering of throw pillows so it wouldn't over(flower)power the room.

My client was adamant about wanting a bright, pretty room reminiscent of an indoor garden, but she also wanted it to be fresh and contemporary. How exactly could I achieve a cozy garden feel without resorting to the froufrou elements of cottage style? Mostly I knew what I didn't want. I nixed floral-pattern upholstery, furniture with distressed paint finishes, needlepoint pillows with tea roses, and— god forbid—dried flower arrangements and wreaths. Yellow Labs shedding on the shabby-chic furniture were also sent to the decorating doghouse.

To start with, I made a backdrop of informal striped walls in alternating shades of acid green, rather than the expected cabbage-rose wallpaper. Bold lime bands like these add soft graphic interest to the room (which lacks architectural details) while creating an outdoorsy garden feel.

Mixing modern, Scandinavian-pop furniture with the homeowner's more traditional items—an antique walnut dresser with filigreed handles, a round pedestal table with a fluted base—tones down the stuffiness of the pedigree pieces. A side table painted full-on pink offers a vibrant contrast to the walls and the inexpensive fiber mats laid end-to-end like carpeting.

The secret to this garden: emphasize the graphic quality of flowers, not the frilliness. Steering clear of anything delicate, nostalgic, or timid, I favored furniture with crisp lines, like the minimalist purple sofa and artwork that made a strong statement, like the yellow canvas with an orange square.

Of course, you can't create a garden fantasia without including some actual vegetation. Fighting the urge to mow the Netherlands, I braved Manhattan's flower market at sunrise to create exuberant displays of mixed blossoms that included tulips and yellow roses, which pull together the room's vivid colors. The result of my horticulture-inspired handiwork is a look that's streamlined, sleek, and fresh as a daisy. Now that's what I call bloom service.

fast fix

Don't attempt to mask a large, empty corner with a fake plant—it just looks like a fake plant trying to mask a large, empty corner. Instead, add vertical interest on the cheap with this simple, urn-topped column made out of white-washed MDF (medium density fiberboard). The urn, while it resembles a costly English antique, is actually a plastic pot from the garden supply store that was disguised with a coat of spray paint. It's sculptural, classic, and only looks expensive.

TURN TO PAGE 182 TO LEARN HOW TO STRIPE YOUR WALLS.

FLOWER POWER

Fresh flowers are a necessity masquerading as a luxury. Lush bouquets or even single stems add life to rooms, not to mention a fragrance more pleasant than any chemical air freshener. While florists offer the widest variety, mass market discounters have unbeatable prices—two dozen roses will set you back less than $15 in most cases. Cut flowers normally last a week in a vase, but hardier varieties like carnations, snapdragons, lilies, chrysanthemums, and foxgloves can make it to the fourteen-day mark if cared for properly. For maximum longevity:

• Recut flowers after purchasing. Slice the stems underwater and on the diagonal.

• Strip off any leaves that are below the water level in the vase. Submerged leaves can rot and breed bacteria.

• Use packets of floral food and change the water daily.

• Keep flowers away from ripening fruit and vegetables, which emit ethylene gas that can cause wilting.

• If the vase is small enough, pop your arrangement in the refrigerator overnight; otherwise, store it in the coldest part of the house.

APPLYING THE PRINCIPLES

FURNITURE PLACEMENT

Rooms with French doors topped with grand-scale arched windows can be a "pane" to decorate. All that sunlight flooding in can fade or rot delicate fabrics, and there needs to be sufficient clearance for the doors to swing open without bumping into the furniture—which shouldn't block the sightline to the view outdoors. Here, a round library table that recalls English manor houses runs circles around those décor dilemmas and instantly becomes the room's focal point. This reproduction is oversized but not intrusive, since there are no sharp angles to impede traffic flow. Since I didn't want any dining connotations, I ringed the table with a quartet of square Ikea ottomans rather than armchairs.

MANAGING CLUTTER

Even though it's expansive, don't let this become a table of contents. Clusters of small tchotchkes atop furniture this size just disappear and lose impact. A better bet: statement-making accessories, like low stacks of glossy gardening books that mimic the shape of the ottomans. A tumultuous riot of flowers in a gargantuan vase (you can also substitute less-costly curly willow or lucky bamboo) bring the garden theme full circle.

CABBAGE PATCH CHIC

No one trumps an Illinois farm family with five boys when it comes to vegetable gardens. We grew everything from beans to carrots to potatoes, and I learned an appreciation for leafy edibles that went way beyond how they tasted: the lush colors of ripe produce provide a vivid palette for decorating, especially in a tiny space like this minuscule dining room. An interior this small requires big ideas—or at least a quirky vegetable-patterned rug. This circular wool carpet, woven with a whimsical design of cabbages, radishes, and snap peas, was an I-can't-believe-I-

found-it score from a home decorating outlet. An irresistible combination of 1930s farmhouse and country kitsch, it became the room's statement piece, with everything growing out of its produce pattern. The eggplant in the weave inspired the sophisticated, purple-black aubergine wall color, and the modern chairs' aqua blue hue was plucked straight from the geometric border. Even the glass-topped dining table was chosen for the unobstructed view it offered of the rug's cauliflower rosette, while the cabbage-leaf place settings and bouquets were obvious references to the vegetables underfoot.

This dining room practically defined the word *cramped.* Tucked away in what amounted to an alcove, it was an awkwardly shaped hexagon chopped up by three doorways—and zero windows. Obviously, a traditional dining suite, with the requisite china cabinet and matching dining table sized for a Viking mead hall, wasn't an option. Neither were staid colors or tired, trite accessories.

Oddly shaped rooms require theatrical drama—like high-contrast colors and furnishings in a mix of styles—so you don't notice the shortcomings. A Swedish-style Ethan Allen buffet adds storage (and underscores the fact that you don't need a hulking hutch or open shelving hovering over you while you eat). The piece's traditional lines look fresh paired

kick start

The nanosecond I spotted this vegetable rug, I flashed back to summer afternoons spent weeding my grandmother Doris's garden. There *is* something old-fashioned and fussy and twee about this carpet. But the fact that it's so unabashedly not in keeping with my usual classic, clean-lined style is what makes it a showstopper—the room minus this high-impact rug would have been a lot less interesting. The same principle applies to any similarly eccentric piece you might inherit or discover in a big box store: work it into your décor by celebrating its difference, and you'll have a visual contrast that will make your existing pieces look that much stronger and more individual.

with glam touches like a gold gilt mirror and rococo brackets. The sly place settings combine blue glass goblets, cabbage-leaf dinnerware, and bamboo-handled flatware in an irreverent combo of classic and contemporary that mimics the veggie rug and the table and chairs.

The final effect of this hallway turned dining room? Part refinement, part rustic, and definitely not garden-variety.

fast fix

Flowers aren't the only option when you're designing a centerpiece. Here, I popped ornamental cabbage and kale into cachepots for an offbeat arrangement. The frilly leaved plants, which look like mutated peonies, are sold at most nurseries in fall and early winter and are available in shades ranging from magenta to creamy green. A pyramid of fresh pears or apples is another easy option.

APPLYING THE PRINCIPLES

PROPORTION AND SCALE

Hanging hefty, rococo wall sconces slightly beyond the edges of the console creates the illusion that this small piece of furniture is longer and larger than it really is. For additional drama, I added an oversized round dining table that's actually a little too large for the space. Its glass top and skinny, swooping legs make it feel airy, not intrusive.

FURNITURE PLACEMENT

Without sharp angles jutting into the space, the round table dramatically softens the surplus of corners in this hexagon-shaped room. The wildly patterned rug, a contrast to the dark purple walls, becomes the room's focal point and dictates the placement of the dining table and chairs.

art of the matter

For less than the cost of mass-produced art-work, you can create your very own Picassos using prestretched and primed canvases from an art supply store—and you'll get exactly the color scheme and subject matter you want. The canvases, which typically range from 3-by-5 inches to 30-by-40 inches (you can also special-order larger sizes), are virtually idiotproof. All you have to do is slap on the paint—acrylics, oils, or even ordinary interior paint is fine—and hang on the wall. Even if you're artistically challenged, you can fake a convincing abstract—why do you think critics of modern art claim a six-year-old could do it?

For the dining room painting, I used a straight-edge to draw a diagonal line across the canvas. The top half I painted sky blue, the bottom half vegetation green, and presto—an instant abstract of the view outside Granny Doris's kitchen. For the Doug Wilson original in the hallway leading to the alcove, I used thinned-down orange paint that I applied in two oppos-ing directions. Then I wiped down the canvas with a damp rag while the paint was still wet. Just call it a baby carrot abstract.

color commentary

Conventional wisdom dictates that in an area this tiny, white is the only logical wall color because it creates an illusion of space. So of course I painted the room eggplant. It might seem counterintuitive, but trust me: When your space is this small, white ain't fooling anybody. Better to go with a statement-making color that adds impact and excitement. Orange, green, or aqua walls would also have played off the carpet's colors, but the result would have been too country-cute. Instead, the regal pur-ple gave the room the metropolitan feel of a posh, urban apartment that just happens to be in the suburbs.

BEADS AND BAUBLES

Renters are often reluctant to spruce up their places in any significant way. If they won't be staying all that long, they figure, why not settle for whatever furnishings are easiest (to cram into moving boxes) and just endure the apartment's shortcomings? Of course, nothing's quite as permanent as a temporary decision that you're still living with a half-decade later. It's all too easy to end up sleeping on a futon and hating the shag carpeting for years on end. My client, a style-conscious attorney, wisely chose to view her tiny

apartment as more than just a run-of-the-mill rental. To the untrained eye, it was a plain vanilla, 1960s studio with a Pullman kitchen and a charmless floor plan that measured less than 500 square feet. But with luxe ethnic touches, a well-edited collection of contemporary furniture, and a few savvy home improvement projects—which rely more on cachet than cash—it was transformed from a diamond in the rough into a dazzling jewel box of an apartment.

It was no surprise that the square parquet flooring and severe angles of this boxy studio threw the owner for a curve. Cartesian regularity like this needs the contrast of soft shapes and irregular forms, which is what the dining alcove is all about. A statement-making round table from West Elm— check out how the open base is constructed from two interlocking ovals—grounds the space without

kick start

One of the perks of living in New York is having free access to some of the world's edgiest interior design. Stroll into various high-end boutiques, lounges, even hair salons, and you can check out hip décor created by the biggest names in the business. Then you can shamelessly rip it off! (Whoever said creativity is the art of concealing your sources knows what I mean.) When my client first spied these beaded curtains at one of her favorite Manhattan restaurants, a gypsy-themed Midtown hotspot designed by famed commercial architect David Rockwell, she knew she had to duplicate them in her own home. The custom curtain, handmade in India to fit the dimensions of the apartment's windows, was constructed from three hundred individual strands of blue glass beads that are weighted at the bottom and hung from a ceiling track. Exotic and elegant, the glittering curtain added a touch of Bollywood chic—in addition to hiding the air conditioning unit—and inspired the wall color and the palette of the Turkish area rug. This one-of-a-kind window treatment was a serious splurge, but since this look is all the raj, you can easily find similar beaded curtains, for far less, at import stores.

out major expense, create unusable alcoves and weird angles that chop up a room's flow.

To hide the abutment and add additional storage, I constructed a faux wall using square panels of inexpensive MDF (medium density fiberboard) coated with polyurethane. This false front, which was placed directly atop the real wall and extends over the alcove, creates a clean, geometric backdrop as well as a series of cubbyholes for stashing clothes and toiletries.

When the lack of space in a studio apartment is driving you out of your mind, built-ins can keep your sanity on track. This versatile made-to-order wall unit, constructed to fit precisely between the kitchen and bedroom, cleverly conceals a stereo and television, plus books, CDs, and out-of-season clothing. Even though it's 103 inches long and 92 inches high, the piece doesn't feel obtrusive, thanks to its clean white finish and recessed bottom. Glass shelving at the end corner lets in light and creates the sense that the objects are floating. Renters are sometimes reluctant to blow the budget on permanent fixtures like this, but the end result can be like a breath of fresh air in cramped quarters.

If your bedroom is on display 24/7—and is fully visible from the dining room—it needs to be a no-holds-barred boudoir, not just a utilitarian place where you crash at the end of the day. Think elegant, understated, with sensuous textures and

weighing it down. Also spot-on: An oversize mirror that runs rings around dinkier looking glasses, undulating curly willow branches, and voluptuous Deco-inspired barware.

Like a lot of rentals, the apartment had an awkward, jutting wall abutment...exactly where I wanted to position the bed. Partial walls like these, which often conceal water pipes or similarly important mechanical stuff that can't be relocated with-

unabashed romance. Here, the only thing missing is the Cole Porter score. Rather than an expected, expensive headboard, which would have clashed with the minimalist paneled wall unit behind it, I opted for over-the-top drama. A jaw-dropping chandelier with dangling crystals the size of plums (a gift from the client's mother) is unexpected and adds visual contrast to the angular bed and cubby-holes. A decadently lush green silk duvet cover with matching pillows and sheets also adds sophis-tication. During dinner parties, the light from the chandelier is reflected in the mirror above the nearby dining alcove's sideboard, setting a posh mood that's anything but bedroom-y.

color commentary

To capitalize on the light streaming in from the east-facing windows, I chose a subtle, tonal wall color that varies depending on the time of day. This beachy, bleached blue-green shade has a soothing, almost underwater feel that sets off the natural-hued upholstery and kiwi-colored bedding. Because the parquet floors were a bland blond and lacked depth—another common problem in rentals—I stained them a tobacco brown to pump up the contrast with the walls. While people sometimes assume that dark floors like this will close in a small space, a rich, deep color underfoot actually warms up a room and creates atmosphere.

APPLYING THE PRINCIPLES

FURNITURE PLACEMENT

Concealing the bed in the semisecluded alcove near the bathroom means it's not visible when you first walk in the door—which helps deemphasize the fact that this is actually a studio apartment.

MANAGING CLUTTER

Since there wasn't room for a dresser in the "bedroom," cubbyholes in the specially built false wall behind the bed provide clothes storage. In the living room, a built-in entertainment unit and banquette cushions that conceal cabinets provide additional spots for storing clutter. Because the open-plan studio lacked walls, the furniture had to work overtime, differentiating the living, eating, and sleeping sections. Bisecting the space and carving out a distinct living room area is a custom-made, L-shaped banquette, wide enough to accommodate overnight guests and to house roomy storage underneath.

SMALL WONDER

Out-of-towners are always shocked to learn that New

Yorkers can fork over thousands a month for an apart-

ment with roughly the dimensions of a walk-in closet

and consider it a bargain. (Those sprawling pads on

Friends? An urban myth.) Of course, most crazy-busy

Manhattanites don't really spend much time at home—

it's mostly a pit stop glimpsed in a blur as they dash in

and out. I'm no exception. Between taping *Trading*

Spaces, lecturing, and doing appearances all over

the country, I'm traveling most of the month, so it's

probably fitting that my Upper East Side apartment

resembles a room in a boutique hotel. (Hey, there's more than one way to be part of the inn crowd.) Tailored furnishings and Deco touches, plus some clever decorating and space solutions, make my 500-square-foot pied-à-terre feel a lot more spacious (seriously) than it really is.

Because it's a railroad apartment—one room leads directly into another, with no hallways—the décor needed to flow seamlessly from the entry to the living room to the bedroom, and I employed a number of visual tricks to create that illusion of continuity.

One route was through color. As a way to help blur the boundaries between rooms, the same brownish-beige, wall-to-wall carpeting is used throughout the space. I also played with variations on the same muted green. For the living room, that meant a grid pattern on the walls using three shades of green; the dark carpet color is then brought up into the trim to help blend the lines and keep the room from feeling choppy. In the bedroom, I pulled the green on the walls and the ceiling straight from the grid in the living room.

I'm guessing the previous renters were nudists, because the apartment had no closets when I first moved in. Instead, there was a single clothes pole running along the back wall. Since that's also where the bedroom was located, every night I'd lie in bed and stare up at the shirts and pants hanging above my head. While it certainly made it easier to plan

kick start

I originally created this unique painted grid pattern for a client. The crisp geometrics are refined and modern, and it was one of my favorite projects. I knew it would work well here because the blocks of three different colors keep the eye moving, so you aren't really sure how big the space is. The grid pattern is also the perfect backdrop for my angular, clean-lined furniture, while the colors are warm and inviting.

APPLYING THE PRINCIPLES

PROPORTION AND SCALE/FURNITURE PLACEMENT

In cramped quarters, orienting the furniture toward the windows creates a feeling of spaciousness, even if the views are less than stellar. Here, that meant all of the room's largest pieces, including the bed, would hug the right-hand wall—potentially creating a lopsided feel to the space. To counter that sensation of listing, I employed a slightly-too-big area rug and an 8-foot-tall artwork as a counterbalance in the bedroom.

LIGHTING

Every accessory counts in a small space, so bland overhead lighting was replaced with Deco-influenced pendant lamps. The fixtures' fluid, romantic lines contrast with the precise furnishings, producing visual tension that livens up the space.

my wardrobe for the next day, it wasn't much to look at.

Finding space for a closet, somehow, was my first priority. It meant sacrificing precious living space, but I carved out a large walk-in closet at the back of the apartment. Outfitted with a dresser, a series of clothes poles, and French closet doors, it became a dressing room and storage area that I could close off from the rest of the room. Placing the bed in what had once been a little-used study was also a smart move. With its fur area rug, Lalique-style glass pendant lamp, and sumptuous Italian bedding, the now-sophisticated bedroom became an extension of the living room, handling guest spillover whenever I entertained.

Custom-made furniture, like the bedroom's bookcase and bed frame, might seem like a splurge, but having pieces constructed to your own specifications can be a money-saver in the long run, since you won't suffer buyer's remorse over less-than-ideal choices. I designed the H-frame bed (a mod sleigh bed) with a headboard slightly lower than standard height, because I didn't want to block the bookcase. The simplicity of the footboard acts as a barrier to the bedroom area and gives the illusion of a partition from the living room. The bookcase I designed grazes the ceiling and hugs every valuable inch of wall space, making the best use of a tight corner. French doors lead to the large walk-in closet at the rear of the bedroom.

TURN TO PAGE 186 TO LEARN HOW
TO MAKE GRID-PATTERN WALLS.

color commentary

New York is a dirty city, and I don't have the time to clean up after it. Leave a window open for a few days, and you'll have so much black soot dusting your apartment that you'd swear there was a smelting plant next door. That's why I chose grime-concealing shades of green, brown, and sand for most of the walls, carpeting, and furniture—and all of the molding—in the apartment. And with paint-encrusted moldings to deal with, I chose to save myself the trouble of stripping them and instead used my decorative painting tricks to create a faux wood finish.

fast fix

Give inexpensive, mass-produced, or unfinished furniture an instant upgrade by adding decorative crown molding and trim. To transform this Ikea bookcase from plain to pedigreed, I staple-gunned a crown cap along the top. Switching the bookcase's style from Scandi-chic mod to refined traditional made it more in keeping with the bedroom's classic décor—with less strain on my budget than a $2,000 high-end designer piece. For even more sophistication, I painted the back of the bookcase's interior a notice-me shade of bright orange.

TURN TO PAGE 184 TO LEARN HOW TO MAKE GILDED DRAWER HANDLES.

art of the matter

All hands on Deco: This three-color grid pattern owes a deco-rating debt to Jean-Michel Frank, the innovative French architect who pioneered Parisian modernism in the 1920s and '30s and influenced scores of subsequent designers, myself included. I captured his appreciation for all things geometric and pared-down with the living room's painted grid—the only artwork the interior needs. To prevent the grid from inducing claustrophobia, I employed a classic decorator's trick to visually expand the narrow space: I hung an oversized mirror above the sofa. The good-looking glass, which I snagged at Manhattan's famed Twenty-sixth Street Flea Market, has swooping Deco lines that I enhanced with off-white paint and silver leafing.

HAUTE CHOCOLATE

Master bedrooms can be battlegrounds, and not just in the obvious ways. Both sexes usually have very distinct ideas about how to decorate this intimate, personal space, probably because they'll be spending a third of their lives there (yeah, yeah, I know they'll be sleeping with their eyes *closed*). If the wife is a frill seeker who wants cozy comfort and florals, and the husband prefers the exact opposite, a full-scale décor war can erupt. But that tension between masculine and feminine design elements can result in unexpected pairings with surprising freshness, like this

bedroom's combination of laid-back luxe and retro modernity.

The homeowners, newlyweds who both work long hours in the publishing business, wanted their master bedroom to be a peaceful haven from their hectic professional lives. They also hoped to unite their often-disparate styles: He's a neatnik with a strict no-clutter policy and a penchant for quirky vintage furniture; she's a recovering pack rat fighting an addiction to shelter magazines who craves Zen simplicity and touches of decadence.

How to reconcile this couple's design sensibilities? Lots of bold colors, catch-all containers as sharp-looking as they are sensible, and quasi-vintage furnishings updated with glam touches, like this 1970s metal dresser. A top-drawer piece found at a flea market, it immediately became the room's focal point after a local auto-body shop powder-coated the stripped steel with a sassy orange that's normally used for car detailing. It's a pricey procedure, but the high-gloss result has such industrial chic—not to mention a twenty-year, no-rust guarantee—that it's worth the splurge.

A secondhand shop yielded the first-rate Thonet chairs, mid-century classics whose potential was covered up by shabby green vinyl upholstery. After an upholsterer refurbished the pair with luxe black-and-white cowhides rounded up on eBay the seating really stands out.

kick start

The homeowners lassoed standout style without ponying up major cash by reupholstering two thrift-store chairs in dramatic black-and-white cowhides. The Thonet originals, clad in 1970s green vinyl and scored for next to nothing at a secondhand furniture shop, immediately went from kitschy to classy after being outfitted in two-toned fur. Of course, just because the chairs could be at home on the range doesn't mean the bedroom required a yee-haw cattle-ranch theme—you don't want guests exclaiming, "Wow! what a rip-roaring Western room!" (And if you do, well, don't ask me to visit or to decorate.) I played against those expectations by emphasizing the chairs' luxe minimalism, which led me to the contemporary color palette.

Because so many of the furnishings and accessories here were brash and attention-grabbing, the room needed a restful bed. But this sleeping beauty, with its ivory leather padding, crisp wooden trim, and geometric lines, is more than just a pretty face: purchased at the Door Store, its cosmopolitan flair is matched by its affordable price tag. To drum up even more visual interest, I flanked the bed with nightstands made from a snare base topped with glass—the perfect marriage of funky and timeless.

art of the matter

You can get a lot for your Monet when you buy artwork at a big box store—if you know what to choose. Steer clear of mass-produced prints, digitally generated faux paintings, and holograms in favor of one-of-a-kind pieces with an artist's signature, like these abstract color studies.

color commentary

While the chocolate walls created a dramatic backdrop for the bedroom's streamlined furnishings, choosing only a neutral palette of browns and beiges would have been too stark and masculine. So I kept the look flirty by adding drapes in a soft robin's-egg blue. This shade, verging on Tiffany's trademark hue, is feminine without being girly, and tones down the testosterone brown; a ceiling the shade of unsalted butter helps the newly added ivory crown molding really pop. And yes, a bedroom should be soothing, but that doesn't mean comatose—which is why I injected spicy pumpkin touches like the dresser and dinnerware.

fast fix

Silk drapes offer a posh pedigree, but what designers often neglect to mention is that this extremely delicate fabric rots after prolonged exposure to sunlight, which is tough to avoid if you're using it as, oh, a window treatment. Leave the tatters to a B-movie mummy's wrappings, and hang faux-silk curtains instead. This practical fabric, usually made from rayon or polyester blends, is easier to care for, looks identical to the stuff spun by silk worms, and won't leave a hole in your wallet—or your drapes.

APPLYING THE PRINCIPLES

PROPORTION AND SCALE

This master bedroom, typical for a house of its age (it was built in 1928), had a quartet of windows in three different, non-standard sizes. To counter the asymmetry, I hung four curtain rods that were all the same length, and as wide as the largest window. This drapery disguise tricks the eye into thinking it's seeing a set of identical windows, and creates a much more balanced feel than a hodgepodge of curtains with mismatched dimensions. Since these lightweight curtains don't need industrial-strength hardware, I actually opted for chunky curtain rods and hefty finials the size of softballs. It's irreverent, and it counterbalances the dresser's gutsy color. The rugged-looking rods and finials (they're actually lightweight plastic) also offer a strong textural contrast to the floaty, diaphanous drapes.

FURNITURE PLACEMENT

To showcase the bedroom's statement-making orange dresser, I positioned it at the spot the eye immediately zeroes in on—the area diagonally opposite the doorway; placing the bed on the east wall kept the traffic pattern flowing in an uninterrupted half-circle from entrance to sitting area to dresser.

PART IV

DO TRY THIS AT HOME

WHEN IT COMES to decorating, some things are better left to the professionals. Glassblowing or stripping lead paint from rotting furniture, to name two, are the kind of projects that should be undertaken only by those with years of experience—and extensive insurance coverage. Almost everything else, from painting, hammering, sewing, refinishing, stapling, stenciling, and wallpapering to tiling, upholstering, and simple wiring, can be successfully completed by regular folks just like you (see any *Trading Spaces* episode). Of course, I can't always be on-site to help with your crafty creations, so this chapter is the next best thing. It's packed with step-

by-step instructions for the projects featured within the pages of *Doug's Rooms*, all illustrated with detailed photographs, and all guaranteed to add some high-impact oomph to your interiors. Even better, these how-to's are as easy on your wallet as they are on your eyes—and none of them require expensive machinery or materials or a million-dollar insurance policy to complete. Just keep in mind that although these projects are practically idiotproof, you should always read the directions carefully before starting, and take necessary safety precautions, like ventilating your work space and notifying your next of kin (joking!).

TISSUE-PAPER WALLS

FOR A CHEAPER, QUICKER VERSION of wallpaper, try this tissue paper technique. If the store-bought color is too bright as it is, you can apply a glaze to tone it down.

YOU'LL NEED a tape measure; 20-by-30-inch sheets of tissue paper; mild dishwashing detergent; matte Mod-Podge; a foam wallpaper roller; a 7-inch roller tray; a 4-inch, soft-bristle flat paintbrush; and clear, latex glaze. If you want to tone down the color with a tinted glaze, you'll also need universal tint in burnt umber; 1 quart oil-based glaze; an edging brush; a container in which to mix the glaze; several sheets of clear acetate or plastic for testing the glaze color and effect on the walls; and a 4-inch natural-bristle staining brush.

1 To determine the amount of tissue paper needed per wall, multiply the wall's height times the width in inches. Now divide this number by the number of square inches in one sheet of tissue paper. Triple that amount so you'll have enough for a second, overlapping layer, cutoffs, and boo-boos. Here, the calculations for a wall measuring 8½ feet high by 10 feet wide, or 102 inches by 120 inches: Wall: $102 \times 120 = 12{,}240$ square inches total. Tissue paper: 20 inches by 30 inches per sheet = 600 square inches per sheet. $12{,}240 \div 600 = 20.4$. Round that up to 21, multiply by 3, and presto—you'll need 63 sheets to cover the wall.

2 You can cut the sheets of tissue into smaller squares and rectangles, like I did (A), or leave them as they are. The smaller sizes are easier to handle, but the cutting and application is more labor intensive.

3 Clean walls with mild detergent and warm water, and wipe down with plain, warm water to remove any soap residue. Let dry completely.

4 With a foam wallpaper roller, apply a thin coat of Mod-Podge onto an area of wall about equal in size to the tissue square you're applying (B). (I used a paintbrush in this photo, which also works well.) Glue down a single sheet of tissue (C), smoothing out major wrinkles with the soft-bristle brush (D), then roll with the foam roller (E). Apply another coat of Mod-Podge to a wall section, and let some of the glue slop over (F) onto the square you just stuck to the wall. Press down another tissue paper square so that it overlaps with the square next to it. Continue, slightly layering and overlapping the squares as you go (G, H), until the wall is covered. Don't worry if the paper wrinkles or puckers slightly—you want the overall effect to look imperfect and hand done. Remember: *flawed to perfection.* Allow the wall to dry overnight.

5 Using the paintbrush, paint the entire wall with latex glaze to seal and protect it and create a soft matte finish.

6 Toning it down: If you need to tone down the color of the wall, mix 3 to 6 drops of the universal tint into 1 quart of oil-based glaze. To test, stipple the glaze on a clear sheet of acetate and hold it up to the wall. For a darker finish, add more tint; to lighten, add more glaze. Lightly stipple the glaze over the walls using a stipple brush.

a

b

c

d

e

f

g

h

NO-SEW WINDOW VALANCE

YOU'LL NEED a piece of ¾-inch plywood measuring 6 inches longer than the width of the window frame and 6 inches wide. (For example, if your window frame measures 44 inches, your plywood should be 50 inches by 6 inches.) In the brown fabric, you'll need three panels each 32 inches long. One panel should be as wide as your plywood frame plus 2 inches; the two other brown panels should be 8 inches wide. In the orange color, which peeks through at the corners, you'll need two panels, each 10 inches by 32 inches. You'll also need an iron; a staple gun; two 4-inch L-brackets (or more for larger windows) plus screws; and iron-in adhesive hemming tape.

TAILORED AND ELEGANT, THIS WINDOW valance doesn't require a stitch of sewing. Now that's what I call window dressing.

1 Cut the five fabric panels to the dimensions specified at left.

2 For each panel, fold a 1-inch hem along the 32-inch side and press with adhesive hemming tape (A, B, C).

3 Fold each panel in half so that all panels are now 16 inches long, and secure with hemming tape (D). The panels should now look like fabric tubes.

4 Lay an orange panel on a clean work surface. Measure 4 inches from the top of the panel, and lightly mark with a pencil or pen line (E).

5 Place the middle of the orange panel onto a front corner of the plywood at the pencil line. The panel should be situated so that 4 inches of excess fabric fall over the side of the plywood, and 4 inches fall over the front of the plywood (F).

6 Staple the orange panel to the plywood. The 4 inches of excess fabric from step 4 should be stapled to the top of the wood (G). At the corners, wrap like a present and staple into place (H). The finished corner should have 12 inches of fabric hanging down, or what designers call a "drop" (I). Repeat with the second orange panel on the other front corner.

7 Staple-gun the brown panels to the front and sides of the plywood. Four inches of the brown fabric should be staple-gunned to the top of the plywood, resulting in a 12-inch drop (J).

8 Attach the L brackets to the underside of the plywood (K). Attach the finished valance above the window (L).

a

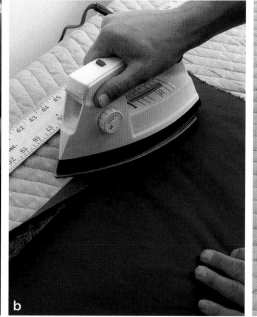

b

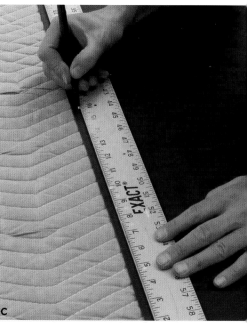

c

d

e

f

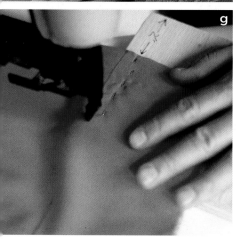

g

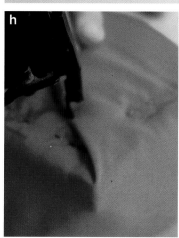

h

i

j

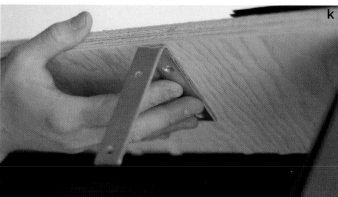

k

l

FABRIC-COVERED FOLDING SCREEN

AN UPHOLSTERED FOLDING SCREEN CAN DO more than just hide clutter—choose a snazzy fabric, and it'll add a jolt of color and pattern to a neutral room. The number and width of the screen's panels can vary depending on what's being concealed (a four-panel screen worked best for my space). I upholstered only one side of this screen, but your divider can do double duty if you cover each side in a different fabric.

YOU'LL NEED four sheets of ¾-inch lightweight MDF (medium density fiberboard), which comes in sheets of 4 feet by 8 feet. (Have the supplier cut the long way in half to give you eight pieces measuring 2 feet by 8 feet.) You'll also need a tube of construction adhesive; a caulk gun; 1¼-inch Sheetrock screws; wood filler; fine-grit sandpaper; tack cloth; 6 yards of fabric (12 if you're covering both sides of the screen); heavy-duty spray-on adhesive; three 6-foot-long piano hinges; 8 Teflon floor glides. You'll need a friend to help you stretch and attach the fabric, and a drill and sander would also be handy.

1 Lay an MDF panel on the floor. Load the adhesive into the caulk gun and squirt lines of glue onto the panel (A). Carefully lay another MDF panel on top of the first panel (B). With a drill, screw the top panel to the bottom panel (C), making sure the screws are sunk below the surface of the MDF. Repeat with the remaining panels.

2 Fill the screw divots with wood filler (D). Let dry.

3 Sand down the wood filler and both sides and the edges of each panel, then wipe down with the tack cloth.

4 Cut the fabric into 4 pieces, each about six inches larger than your panels.

5 Using scrap wood and extra fabric, practice applying the spray-on adhesive to the wood and placing the fabric over it. You don't want to use so much adhesive that it soaks through the fabric. When you think you've got it right, coat the top and sides of one MDF panel with spray adhesive (E).

6 With a friend helping, stretch a fabric panel taut (F) and position atop the MDF (G). Tuck the fabric down along the sides (for the corners, follow the same technique that you would use to wrap a present) (H, I). Smooth out any wrinkles in the fabric, and let the adhesive dry for a few hours. Flip the MDF panel over, and neatly trim away any excess fabric. Repeat with the remaining panels and the opposite sides, if you are covering both sides.

7 Attach the panels together with the piano hinges (J). Make sure the middle hinge opens in a direction opposite to the two outside hinges, so the screen will fold accordion style (J, K).

8 Add two Teflon floor glides to the underside of each panel.

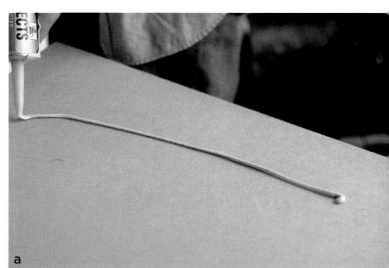

"ANTIQUE" WICKER BASKETS

WHILE THE PRICES AT MASS-MARKET DECORATING stores are unbeatable, sometimes the wares can seem a little too mass-produced. I loved the sturdiness and size of these baskets, but the lacquer finish was too shiny for my taste. So I created instant personality by artificially aging the baskets with brown paint. Using a few different dark colors with the same process will give more depth and character, and you'll find this easy technique works on almost any type of wicker.

YOU'LL NEED baskets; fine-grit sandpaper; tack cloth; a medium-size paintbrush; Behr's Chocolate Sparkle (770B-70) and/or variations thereof; rags; and clear varnish or glaze, if desired.

1 Lightly sand the baskets to roughen the surface. Wipe them off thoroughly using the tack cloth.

2 Apply a semithick coat of paint (A), then randomly dab it off with a rag (B). Don't try for precision or symmetry when you're removing the paint —the more slapdash it looks, the better. You can even sand the baskets a little after rubbing off paint for more interest and depth.

3 Let the paint dry completely. If you like, brush on a coat of clear varnish or glaze to seal the finish and prevent it from fading or rubbing off.

Tip: This technique can be used to age all sorts of art and accessories. Also try using other products to age, such as Old English scratch and dent polish, artist's oil paints, and wood stains. Just be sure to put a sealer on the finished product.

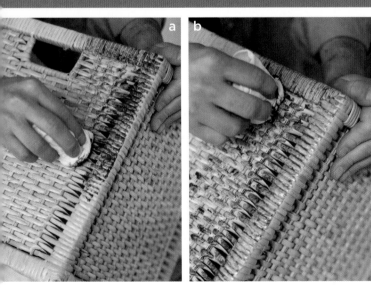

TWEED DRESSER

COVERED IN NUBBY TWEED, THIS DRESSER IS AN homage to Coco Chanel (1883–1971), the rule-flouting visionary who revolutionized women's fashion with her streamlined little black dress, costume jewelry, and cardigan sweaters. Chanel, whose signature colors were black and white, is credited with creating the first two-piece tweed suit for gals, after influential trips to Scotland in the late 1920s with the Duke of Westminster. Now, Chanel tweeds and wool bouclés are as iconic as double-C buttons and quilted, chain-strapped purses—and look equally striking when outfitting furniture.

I used a Chanel-style wool suiting fabric to cover Ikea's "Bialitt" dresser. Because it has wide drawers, no hardware, and comes unassembled, it is particularly well "suited" to the task. You can substitute another dresser as long as it has clean lines and can be taken apart easily.

Tip: Before gluing down the fabric, note the location of the screw holes. Lightly mark with a pencil the position of each hole. Puncture each pencil mark with the utility knife. The knife needs to be extremely sharp if you want a clean cut, so remember to change the breakaway blades frequently during this project.

1 Lay the dresser top, sides, and drawer fronts on a clean work surface (A). Cut a fabric piece large enough to cover the dresser top, then repeat with the sides and drawer fronts (B).

2 Using scrap wood and extra fabric, practice applying the spray-on adhesive to the wood and placing the fabric over it. You don't want to use so much adhesive that it soaks through the fabric. When you're ready . . .

YOU'LL NEED an unassembled dresser; enough tweed fabric to cover all exterior surfaces of the dresser, plus a fourth again as much to allow for matching, folding, and overage (I used about 4 yards); heavy-duty spray-on adhesive; a wallpaper roller; and a utility knife with breakaway blades.

3 Coat all the dresser pieces completely with adhesive (C, D, E).

4 Position the fabric over the dresser pieces, making sure the lines in the tweed are straight. Glue down the fabric (F, G).

5 Smooth any wrinkles by briskly rolling the wallpaper roller over the fabric (H). Press down the fabric firmly near the corners (I).

6 Now fold the fabric around the corners (J). Use the same technique that you would use to wrap presents (K). Make sure that you completely wrap all sides of the legs (L).

7 Trim off any excess fabric (M). For the closest fit, you may have to pull the fabric taut before you snip it off (N, O). Realign stripes if necessary.

8 Assemble the dresser after the adhesive has dried (P).

c

d

e

i

j

k

p

STENCILED CURTAINS

Stenciling is one of the easiest ways to upgrade the look of inexpensive fabrics. Here, ordinary burlap used in gardens and plant nurseries, and usually available for less than $3 a yard, became sophisticated with a repeating fern motif. Try the same technique on muslin, cotton remnants, or even painter's drop cloths.

Tip: Occasionally wipe down the acetate stencil with the damp sponge to remove any wet or drying paint. You may also have to spray additional adhesive onto the acetate if it's no longer sticking firmly to the fabric.

YOU'LL NEED a utility knife; a fern stencil; 1 sheet of clear acetate; spray-on adhesive; an iron; washed fabric curtains; fabric paint; paper plates; a stencil brush; a damp sponge; and paper towels.

1 With the utility knife, cut out the design of your stencil.

2 Lightly coat one side of the stencil with spray adhesive until the paper is tacky. Mount the stencil onto the acetate. Pressing firmly with the utility knife, cut out the pattern. Slice through the acetate as cleanly as you can to create the smoothest possible edges. Peel off any paper remaining on the acetate.

3 Iron the curtains and lay them flat on a clean work surface. If your fabric has some stretch to it, you may need to anchor the curtains—try soup cans—to keep the fabric as flat as possible.

4 Lightly coat the back of the acetate stencil with the spray-on adhesive just until it's tacky. Position it onto the fabric (A).

5 Pour a few tablespoons of the fabric paint onto a paper plate. Dip the stencil brush lightly into the paint and blot the brush by dabbing it on paper towels. Try to have the least amount of paint on your brush as possible—if the brush is too wet, excess paint will seep underneath the acetate and blur the design.

6 Using a stippling, or dabbing up-and-down action, apply the paint inside the stencil design, being sure to cover the edges (B). Remove the stencil before the paint dries and move it to the next area to be stenciled (C).

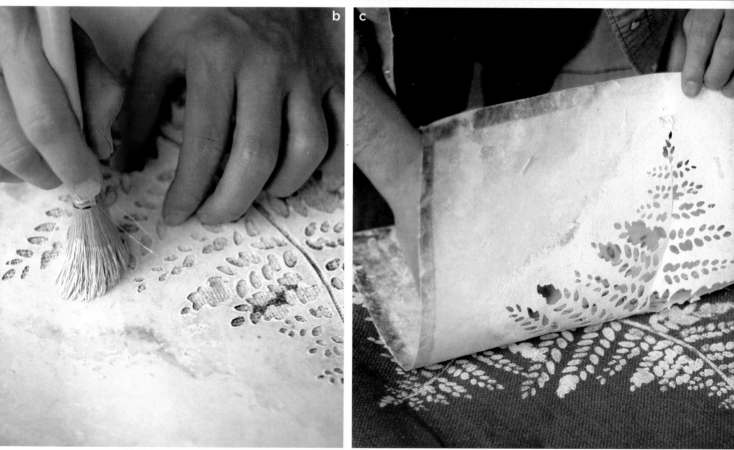

BARK PAPER CEILING

Bark paper, a designer favorite that is as ecologically correct as it is stunning, added rough-hewn texture to the dining room's ceiling. This irregularly grained paper, handmade by the Otomi Indians of Mexico, is created without machinery or chemicals in a process virtually unchanged since the heyday of the Aztecs five hundred years ago. It's nubby and tactile, and comes in assorted weights, from crepe paper thin to poster board thick.

For this ceiling, I used a medium-weight paper in a marble shade. Dyed bark paper is also available if you want a color other than the natural brown. Remember that since each sheet of bark paper is different, the finished ceiling won't be uniform in color or texture.

Tip: Base coat the ceiling in a paint color that matches the overall tone of your bark paper, so that any gaps between sheets will blend. And no, this is not cheating; it's how the pros work!

1 Determine the amount of bark paper you'll need by multipling the ceiling's length times the width in inches. Divide this number by the number of square inches in a single sheet of the bark paper you will be using. With the utility knife and straight-edge, cut the bark paper to the size and number of squares you need (A, B).

2 Apply Roman's R-35 wallpaper prep or sizing to a small portion of the ceiling and let dry.

3 Find the center point of your ceiling by drawing diagonal lines or snapping a chalk line from corner to corner, to form an X in the middle of the ceiling. The intersection of the X is the center point (C).

YOU'LL NEED a tape measure; bark paper (to determine the quantity, see step 1); Roman's R-35 wallpaper prep or sizing; premixed wallpaper glue; a paint-roller tray; a paint roller; an angled paintbrush; a damp sponge; a plastic smoother; a utility knife; and a straight edge.

4 Place a bark square pattern-side down on a clean work surface. Pour the premixed glue into the paint-roller tray, and using the paint roller or brush, apply the glue to the bark paper (D). Try for a thin, even coat of glue without clumps or bubbles. Let the glue set according to package directions (usually a few minutes depending on the brand), then wipe off excess with the sponge.

5 At the ceiling's center point, position the square over the center so that the points of the paper touch the lines created by your pencil or chalk line (E). Smooth the paper lightly with your hands, flattening any wrinkles with the plastic smoother.

6 Moving clockwise, position the next square as shown below (F). Glue on successive squares, constantly moving in a clockwise pattern (G). As you get close to the walls, you may find it easier to apply the glue with the angled brush rather than the roller.

7 Using the utility knife and the straightedge, trim any excess paper that hangs down over the walls. Don't worry if the ceiling doesn't look perfect—the effect you're after here is rustic, not polished. Remember: Flawed to perfection.

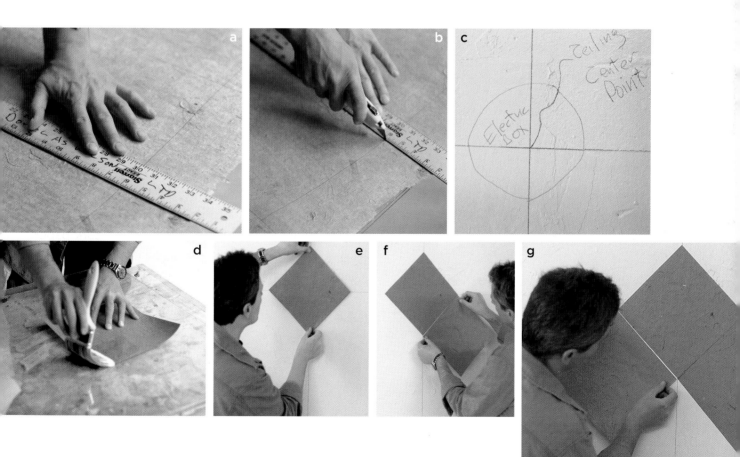

PAINTED LAMP

The secret to the lacquerlike finish on this painted lamp? An aerosol sprayer, which can transform any type of paint into a fine, even mist. Available at most craft or paint stores for less than $15, the sprayer includes a 6-ounce glass jar that you fill with paint—just remember to clean thoroughly before switching colors. Using steady pressure and a controlled back-and-forth motion will prevent drips and yield the slickest look possible.

YOU'LL NEED a lamp; fine-grit sandpaper; a tack cloth; an oil-based spray primer; paint thinner; an aerosol sprayer; 1 quart white satin oil paint; 1 quart red satin oil paint; painter's tape; and spray-on polyurethane.

1 Remove the lamp shade. Thoroughly sand the lamp base, then wipe it with the tack cloth.

2 Prime the lamp with the oil-based spray primer; let it dry, then lightly sand it smooth and wipe down with the tack cloth.

3 Fill the aerosol sprayer with thinned white satin oil paint and lightly spray the entire lamp. Let it dry overnight, then sand and wipe it with the tack cloth. Using the aerosol sprayer, apply as many coats of paint as are necessary for complete coverage, and let the lamp dry for 24 hours.

4 Tape off the portions of the lamp that you want to remain white (A). Fill the aerosol sprayer with thinned red satin oil paint and lightly spray the entire lamp (B). Let it dry, then sand and wipe it with the tack cloth. Again, apply as many coats of paint as are necessary for complete coverage. Let dry thoroughly, at least 24 hours. Remove the tape.

5 Protect the finish with multiple coats of spray-on polyurethane.

a b

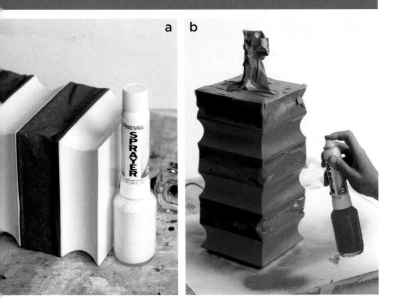

STRIPED LAMP SHADES

Add graphic sass to zero-personality white lamp shades with these graduated red stripes. I used the same eggshell interior paint that was applied to the walls but a high-gloss, oil-based paint would work just as well—plus give the shade a shimmery sheen.

YOU'LL NEED a white paper lamp shade; a tape measure; painter's tape; paint; and a small or medium-size foam paintbrush, depending on the size of your shade.

1 Determine the number of stripes you want on your lampshade. Measure the top circumference of the shade. Divide this top circumference by the number of stripes. Say you want 15 narrow stripes, and the shade's top circumference is 30 inches. 30 ÷ 15 = 2. So 2 inches will be the stripe width at the top of the shade. With light pencil marks, measure 2-inch increments at the top of the shade.

2 Repeat for the shade's bottom circumference to get the width of the stripe at the bottom of the shade, but don't mark those off yet. (If the bottom circumference is 45 inches, then 45 ÷ 15 stripes = 3 inches.)

3 Now draw a single, perpendicular line from one of the shade's top markings to the bottom of the shade. From that bottom mark, repeat step 1, measuring increments the width of the bottom part of the stripe.

4 Draw lines connecting the top and bottom stripe-width markings (A). Tape off the area between the stripes to be painted (B).

5 Paint each stripe, and apply a second coat if necessary (C). Let the paint dry completely between coats. Remove the tape while the second coat of paint is still wet (D).

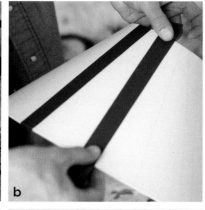

a   b

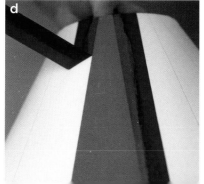

c   d

CHINOISERIE MURAL

IF YOU'VE AVOIDED PAINTING A MURAL BECAUSE you were scared off by the difficulty or the expense, this Asian landscape is for you. The secret is that elementary school staple, the overhead projector: just shine the drawing onto the wall, trace the image in chalk, then go over it with paint. For the best results, choose a simple black-and-white drawing with clean lines, like this chinoiserie sketch I found in a vintage art book. But note that you can use this technique for any design. Be creative! There are literally hundreds of images to choose from on clip art CD-roms, which also have the advantage of being in the public domain, so you don't have to worry about copyright laws. An overhead projector can usually be rented from a library or church, or you can purchase one for about $100 at an office supply store.

YOU'LL NEED a line drawing as your mural motif; transparency film; a transparency pen; an overhead projector; white chalk; a calligraphy brush; paint for desired wall color; and white eggshell house paint.

1 Clean and prime the walls. Let the primer dry completely. Paint the walls with the color you've chosen for the mural's background (A). I used Behr's Pointsettia 150B-7.

2 To make the transparency, place the transparency film on top of the line drawing and trace over it using the transparency pen. Or you can have a copy shop photocopy the drawing onto the transparency film for you.

3 Use the overhead projector to shine the image onto the wall (B). The distance of the projector from the wall determines the size of the image, so you'll probably need to move the projector back and forth until you land on the mural dimensions that look best.

4 Trace the projected image on the wall using white chalk, making sure not to jostle or move the projector (C).

5 Dip the calligraphy brush in the white paint, and paint as close to the chalk drawing as you can, without tracing directly over it. Use short, quick strokes to achieve nice wispy effects and tendrils (D, E).

STRIPED WALLS

PAINTING HORIZONTAL STRIPES ON A WALL CAN add architectural interest and make the space feel bigger. The width of the stripes should vary according to the height of the walls—to counterbalance this room's 9-foot walls, I used 12-inch stripes. Your stripes shouldn't be any narrower than 4 inches or any wider than 12 inches.

1 Clean the walls using a mixture of 2 tablespoons mild dishwashing detergent to 1 gallon of warm water. Let them dry, then wipe down with plain, warm water to remove any soap residue.

2 Tape off window and door frames and trim with painter's tape.

3 Prime the walls. Use the roller for the largest areas and the edging brush for trim. Let the primer dry completely.

4 Paint all four walls Japanese Fern, the base color. Let the paint dry, preferably overnight. Apply a second coat of Japanese Fern, and let it dry overnight.

5 Starting at the baseboard, using the level (A, B) and straightedge (C), mark the wall lightly with pencil where your stripes will be (D). Starting again at the baseboard, tape off every other stripe on the stripe's outside perimeter (E).

6 Paint the stripes Lemon Grass. Let them dry completely. Apply a second coat of Lemon Grass, and remove the tape while the paint is still wet (G).

YOU'LL NEED mild dishwashing detergent; painter's tape; primer; paint rollers; a paint roller tray; a fine soft-bristle edging brush; Behr's Japanese Fern 400B-6; Behr's Lemon Grass 400-B7; a level; and a straightedge.

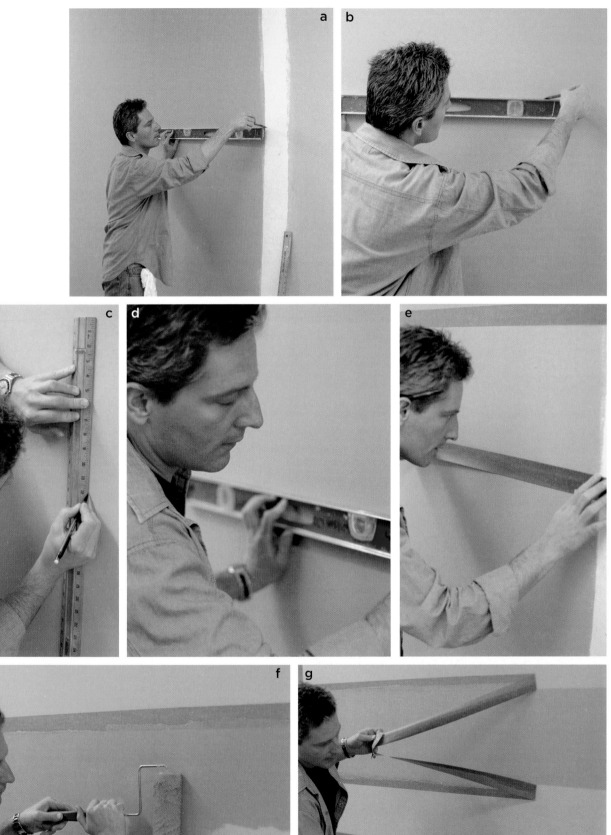

GILDED DRAWER HANDLES

GILDING IS A TECHNIQUE IN WHICH ULTRATHIN sheets of silver or gold are overlaid onto an object. The process, also called leafing, is a little tricky because the fragile metal sheets measure only five millionths of an inch thick. Since they're easily crinkled and torn, do this project away from drafts and breezes. Also, the oils in your hands will tarnish the silver, so I don't recommended silver leafing for bathroom or kitchen handles. Other than that, there's no limit to your gilt complex.

Tip: For best results apply the leafing with a gilder's tip, a three-inch-wide brush made from super-fine squirrel or camel's hair. It's a stroke of genius when it comes time to pick up a single sheet of leafing: Just rub the gilder's tip back and forth across your arm hair, and the static electricity that's generated will grab the leaf like a magnet.

YOU'LL NEED denatured alcohol; cotton rags; latex gloves; spray-on sizing adhesive; silver leafing sheets; a gilder's tip (see Tip, right); and spray polyurethane. You can also use a silver leafing kit, which usually includes leafing sheets, adhesive, a gilder's tip, and a burnishing cloth.

1 Thoroughly clean the handles using the denatured alcohol and the cotton rags (A).

2 Spray adhesive on to the handle (B). Wearing latex gloves, use the gilder's tip to pick up a silver leaf. Carefully press a sheet of silver over the handle (C). Don't worry if the sheets tear or crumble—just apply additional sheets or pieces until the entire handle is covered. Let dry.

3 Using the gilder's tip, lightly brush away any silver crumbs or particles from the handles (D). I actually used a soft-bristle paintbrush in this photo, but I've been doing this for years.

4 To protect and seal the finish, apply two or three coats of spray polyurethane, making sure to let the handles dry between coats.

a

b

c

d

GRID-PATTERN WALLS

THIS PAINTED GRID PATTERN IS A GREAT WAY TO enliven a room that lacks architectural details. Since it's so bold, you may want to use it on just a single wall. You'll use three complementary colors to create the 24-inch-by-24-inch squares of the grid: a light green, a dark green, and a mixed green that's a fifty-fifty combination of each.

Keep in mind that depending on the height and width of your walls, you'll probably need to adjust the grid pattern slightly. If your wall measurements can't be evenly divided by 24, you'll have to fudge the size of the squares a little. Always, always, always make the blocks at the top center of the wall a perfect square, and add any excess or deletions to the blocks on the farthest left and farthest right of the row. This works best when the difference is minimal. But say your wall measures 13 feet long, or 156 inches. 156 divided by 24 is 6.5. So you have six and a half 24-inch squares. That extra half square measures 12 inches, which means you'll have 6 additional inches at either end of the wall. This may be a little too much overage.

Another way to approach the same 13-foot wall is to distribute the 12 inches overage equally among all the squares. If you want a total of six squares, divide 6 into 156 (the width of wall), which gives you 26. So instead of six and a half 24-inch squares, you'll have six 26-inch squares. Remember, people: this is an art, not a science, so you're gonna have to be a little creative here.

1 Clean the wall or walls with 2 tablespoons of mild dishwashing detergent in 1 gallon of warm water. Let dry, then wipe down with plain, warm water to remove any soap residue.

2 Tape off trim and the window and door frames.

3 Prime the wall using the roller for the largest areas and painting in a W-shaped pattern for best coverage . . . just get the wall painted. Let the primer dry completely.

4 Combine equal parts of the light green and the dark green to create the mixed green (A), and paint the entire wall using the darkest shade of green.

5 Measure the height and width of the wall, and divide by the number of 24-inch (or whatever works best for your dimensions—see the examples on the previous page) horizontal and vertical rows that you want. Use the chalk and level to mark your lines.

6 Starting at the top square on the top left row, tape off every second or third square (B, C).

7 Paint the taped-off squares with the light green and the dark green paint, using whatever color configuration you like, as long as no two successive squares are the same color (D).

8 Allow the squares to dry, then apply a second coat, and remove the tape while the paint is still wet (E).

9 When all is dry, wipe off any telltale chalk lines and enjoy your finished grid (F).

b

c

d

e

f

HOW TO MAKE A PADDED HEADBOARD

THE BEAUTY OF THIS PADDED HEADBOARD is that the design can be easily modified to fit a room's personality. Since I wanted a minimalist look with clean lines, I opted for a mid-height headboard, but you can make yours as tall as you'd like. Keep in mind that the headboard will inevitably become soiled—even freshly washed hair contains oils that will cause staining—so choose a heavier-weight fabric that can be spot cleaned, rather than something delicate like silk or suede.

Tip: For an even more tailored look, trim the headboard with a wood border. Here, I used 2-inch-by-2-inch oak stained mahoghany brown (G). You can either nail the border directly into the plywood, or just nail it directly into the wall around the headboard.

YOU'LL NEED a tape measure; ¾-inch plywood; ¾-inch batting, available at fabric stores; 3 to 6 yards of fabric depending on the size of your headboard; and a staple gun.

1 To determine the width of your padded headboard, measure the width of your bed. The height can be whatever you like—you can even extend the headboard all the way to the ceiling for a funky, Alice-in-Wonderland effect. Have the lumberyard cut the plywood to your desired dimensions.

2 Lay the roll of batting down on a clean work surface and place the plywood on top (A).

3 Trim the batting so it's only 3 inches larger than the plywood (B). Fold the batting over onto the plywood, and attach with a staplegun (C, D).

4 Place the headboard batting-side down on the back side of the fabric. If necessary, trim the fabric so that it extends just 6 inches beyond the plywood. Pulling the fabric taut but not so tight that it puckers and pulls, fold it over the edges of the plywood and staple securely into place (E, F).

RESOURCES

Products featured in *Doug's Rooms* (see following page for information regarding sources).

Vacation Memories, page 59
Sofa: Door Store

Silk Leaf, page 60
Wooden blinds: Smith + Noble; **kitchen buffet:** Ballard Designs; **dinnerware:** Horchow.

Pitcher, page 61
Rug: Home Decorators Collection; **chandelier:** Maxim Lighting International.

Box of Chocolates, page 62
Sequin pillow cover, nesting tables: West Elm; **bed, lamp:** Ikea

Aroma of Chai Tea, page 63
Chair: Ikea.

Striped Handbag, page 64
Light fixture: Maxim Lighting International; **chair and ottoman:** Room & Board

Woman's Scarf, page 65
Sofas: Room & Board; **chandelier:** Maxim Lighting International; **armoire:** Ethan Allen.

Cheeky Tiki, pages 70–79
Tissue paper: S. Walter Packaging; **lamps, couch, coffee table, CD storage boxes, vases in bookcase, desk organizer, orange pillows, tic-tac-toe, dominoes:** Crate & Barrel; **bookcases, baskets:** Ikea; **rug, throw, multicolored pillow:** ABC Carpet & Home; **cookie jar:** Marshalls; **divider:** AJO Lumber & Woodworking; **vase on table:** T.J. Maxx; **bracket:** HomeGoods; **fabric:** Mood Apparel; **glass vase:** Ross Dress for Less; **brown pillows:** National Wholesale Liquidators; **bamboo shades:** Smith + Noble; **canvases:** Michaels; **television:** J&R; **chairs, glass table, side table:** Doug's own; **yellow pillows:** Bed Bath & Beyond; **custom artwork:** Doug Wilson.

French Twist, pages 80–89
Glass end tables: Ethan Allen; **black and white tables, dresser, white curtains:** Ikea; **rug:** Home Decorators Collection; **white chickens:** Target; **black-and-white chickens:** Michaels; **tornado prints, frames:** Spectra Photo; **brackets, black leather pillows, glass lamp:** HomeGoods; **couch, black lamps, leather chair, mirror:** Housing Works Thrift Shop; **throw, vase, boxes:** T.J. Maxx; **small white chicken:** eBay; **hot pink linen fabric made into curtains and pillows:** Amin Fabric; **tornado images:** Weatherstock; **custom-designed H-benches:** Doug's own

Central Bark, pages 90–97
Bark paper: Caba Paper; **glass vases:** Pottery Barn; **shades:** Smith + Noble; **burlap fabric, green fabric:** NY Elegant Fabrics; **Akari fixture:** Pearl River Mart; **hurricanes, console table, cornucopia:** Crate & Barrel; **dining table:** Bergen Office Furniture; **chairs:** client's own; leaf prints, **green fabric:** Spectra Photo; **candles:** T.J. Maxx; **wood frame:** Ikea

Asian Fusion, pages 98–105
Swing, side tables, coffee table, armchairs, east chairs, sheepskin throws, cabinet, candle: Ikea; **porcelain figures (cranes, dog, turtle, cat):** Man Hing Imports; **glass lamps, brackets:** HomeGoods; **Asian goddess head, red-and-white custom-painted lamps, glass vase:** T.J. Maxx; **mirror:** Malmaison Antiques; **tea set, bowl, fortune cookies, sake bottle:** Pearl River Mart; **glass bowl, sheepskin pillows, shaker, tray, martini glasses, toothpick holder:** Pottery Barn; **red brocade fabrics:** Amin Fabric

Posh Pucci, pages 106–115
Bathroom and kitchen tile, bathroom sink: Artistic Tile; **bathroom and kitchen fittings and accessories:** Dornbracht; **toilet:** Toto; **bathtub:** Bain Ultra; **custom wall unit, vanity, banquette, bedside tables:** Benchmark Woodworking; **banquette fabric:** NY Elegant Fabrics; **blue-and-white round vases:** HomeGoods; **sofa, side chair:** Sofa So Good; **artwork below television:** Michele D'Ermo; **coffee table, dresser:** client's own; **rug, Matteo bedding:** ABC Carpet & Home; **bedside table lamps, mirror:** Crate & Barrel; **yellow-and-white pillows:** Sheila Sculley Designs; **Lucite chairs:** Unica Home; **custom artwork above sofa, custom headboard:** Doug's own; **artwork in kitchen:** Nuala Clarke & Jimmie James; **shades:** Smith + Noble; **television:** Sound City; **artwork on page 27:** Sally Egbert.

Heavy Petal, pages 116–125
Dining table, side tables: Ethan Allen; **stools, chairs, sofa, coffee table, sisal rugs:** Ikea; **custom pedestals:** AJO Lumber & Woodworking; **brackets, obelisk, lamps, watering can, throw, dogs, decorative acorn:** HomeGoods; **candles:** Target; **hurricanes:** Pier 1 Imports; **hot pink and floral fabric for curtains and pillows:** Amin Fabric; **framed tulip print:** J. Pocker & Sons; **vases:** Pottery Barn; **mirror:** T.J. Maxx; **custom artwork:** Doug Wilson; **canvas:** Pearl Paint; **urns:** Nature's Foliage & Gardens.

Cabbage Patch, pages 126–133
Rug: HomeGoods; **bamboo flatware:** eBay; **goblets, candleholders:** Pottery Barn; **hurricanes:** Pier 1 Imports; **buffet:** Ethan Allen; **chairs:** Nuovo Melodrome; **brackets, mirror:** T.J. Maxx; **cabbage plates and bowls:** Marshalls; **cabbage tureen, napkins:** Williams-Sonoma; **table:** ABC Carpet & Home; **candles:** Target; **custom artwork:** Doug Wilson; **canvas:** Pearl Paint.

Beads and Baubles, pages 134–141
Standing lamps, console, shaker, ice bucket, wine cooler, bedside rug: Ikea; **candles, throw, pillows with circles:** Target; **mirror:** Straight from the Crate; **white vase, small brown vase and bowl on coffee table:** Daffy's; **bedside table:** Housing Works Thrift Shop; **banquette, entertainment/wall unit:** Benchmark Woodworking; **dining table, chairs:** West Elm; **beige fabric on banquette cushions:** Mood Apparel; **glass coffee table:** Siglo XX; **white vase:** Marshalls;

bedding, small check pillows: Maurice Villency; desk: Door Store; desk chair: Ballard Designs; glasses, glass vases, dinnerware, flatware, candle holders, brown decorative bowl, chandelier, statue: client's own; table lamp: HomeGoods; shades: Smith + Noble; large brown vase, brown-and-white striped vase: Pier 1 Imports; area rug: ABC Carpet & Home.

Small Wonder, pages 142–151
Sofa, chairs, cabinet, lamps: Crate & Barrel; Signoria bedding, carpet, pillows, square mirror: ABC Carpet & Home; shades: Smith + Noble; bookcase, French doors: AJO Lumber & Woodworking; glass top coffee table, end tables:

Housing Works Thrift Shop; bedside table: Debbie's Stamford Antiques Center; sheepskin rug: Cloud Nine Sheepskin; bowls, vase: Eziba.

Haute Chocolate, pages 152–159
Bed frame: Door Store; dresser, chairs: clients own; mirrors, brown pillows: Ikea; bedside tables, coffee table: Straight from the Crate; lamps, aqua pillows, vases, magazine basket, basket with lid, plates: HomeGoods; coffee mugs, napkins: Crate & Barrel; bedding: Chambers; curtain fabric: NY Elegant Fabrics; rug, throw: ABC Carpet & Home; stackable nesting tables: West Elm; framed artwork: Expo Design Center

ABC Carpet & Home
212-473-3000

AJO Lumber & Woodworking
212-749-3632

Amin Fabric
212-764-5184

Artistic Tile
www.artistictile.com

Bain Ultra
www.bainultra.com

Ballard Designs
www.ballarddesigns.com

Bed Bath & Beyond
www.bedbathandbeyond.com

Benchmark Woodworking
973-925-8228

Bergen Office Furniture
www.bergenofficefurniture.com

Caba Paper
www.handmadepapers.com

Chambers
800-840-2870

Nuala Clarke & Jimmie James
917-628-4276

Cloud Nine Sheepskin
www.sheepskin.com

Crate & Barrel
www.crateandbarrel.com

Daffy's
www.daffys.com

Debbie's Stamford Antiques Center
888-329-3546

Michele D'Ermo
631-324-6693

Door Store
www.doorstorefurniture.com

Dornbracht
www.dornbracht.com
eBay
www.ebay.com

Sally Egbert
212-643-4216

Ethan Allen
www.ethanallen.com

Expo Design Center
www.expo.com

Eziba
www.eziba.com

Home Decorators Collection
www.homedecorators.com

HomeGoods
www.tjx.com/about/home-goods.html

Horchow
www.horchow.com

Housing Works Thrift Shop
www.housingworks.org/thrift

Ikea
www.ikea.com

J&R
www.jandr.com

Malmaison Antiques
212-288-7569

Man Hing Imports
212-684-5090

Marshalls
www.marshallsonline.com

Maurice Villency
www.mauricevillency.com

Maxim Lighting International
www.maximlighting.com

Michaels
www.michaels.com

Mood Apparel
212-730-5003
National Wholesale Liquidators
www.nationalwholesaleliquidators.com

Nature's Foliage & Gardens
212-268-0381

NY Elegant Fabrics, Inc.
212-302-4984

Nuovo Melodrome
212-219-0013

Pearl Paint
www.pearlpaint.com

Pearl River Mart
212-431-4770

Pier 1 Imports
www.pier1.com

J. Pocker & Sons
www.jpocker.com

Pottery Barn
www.potterybarn.com

Room & Board
www.roomandboard.com

Ross Dress for Less
www.rossstores.com

Sheila Sculley Designs
212-741-0530

Siglo XX
www.sigloxxnyc.com

Smith + Noble
www.smithnoble.com

Sofa So Good
212-219-8860

Sound City
www.soundcity.com

Spectra Photo
www.spectraphoto.com

Straight from the Crate
www.straightfromthecrate.com

Target
www.target.com

T.J. Maxx
www.tjmaxx.com

TOTO
www.totousa.com

Unica Home
www.unicahome.com

S. Walter Packaging Corp.
www.swalter.com

Weatherstock
www.weatherstock.com

West Elm
www.westelm.com

Williams-Sonoma
www.williamsonoma.com

My other favorite sources I turn to again and again:

California Closets
www.californiaclosets.com

The Home Depot
www.thehomedepot.com

INDEX

apartments, 106–15, 134–51
artwork, 23, 24, 76, 88, 133, 151, 156

banquettes, 109, 141
baskets, "antique" wicker, 170
bathrooms, 51, 112
bedrooms, 23, 62, 63, 113–14, 138–41, 152–59
beds, 114, 146, 156, 188–89
benches, storage, 51
black colors, 88
blue colors, 35, 110, 139, 157
bookcases, 50, 73–74, 146, 150
brown colors, 157
buffet tables, 129–30

cabinets, kitchen, 115
carpets, 101, 145
ceilings, 73, 79, 112–13, 176–77
chairs, 94, 155
closets, 31, 145–46
clutter management, 46–51
　　bedrooms, 141
　　dining areas, 113
　　discarding clutter, 48
　　family rooms, 104
　　living rooms, 113
　　office spaces, 77
　　organizing solutions, 48–51
　　sitting rooms, 125
coffee tables, 77, 84
color schemes, 32–39. See also specific colors
　　deciding, 34–37
　　paint types, 38–39
couches, 24, 86
curtains, 25, 137, 157, 158, 174–75

dining areas, 90–97, 109, 126–33, 137–38
dining tables, 94, 97, 130, 137–38
doors, French, 125
doorways, 31
drapes, 25, 93–94, 157
drawer handles, gilded, 184–85
dressers, 155, 171–73

entryways, 51

family rooms, 49, 98–105
fireplaces, 28
flooring, 101, 113, 139, 145
flowers, 121, 122
focal points, 28, 86, 125, 130, 155
folding screens, 77, 168–69
furniture. See also furniture placement; specific furniture
　　built-ins, 138
　　buying tips, 84
　　customizing, 150
　　custom-made, 146
　　proportion and scale, 23
furniture placement, 26–31
　　bedrooms, 141, 146, 158
　　common problems, 31
　　dining rooms, 97, 130
　　factors to consider, 28–29
　　family rooms, 104
　　living rooms, 86, 113
　　sitting rooms, 125

green colors, 36, 119, 139, 149

headboards, padded, 114, 188–89

inspirations, 56–65
intimate areas, creating, 28–29

kitchens, 50, 60, 114–15

lamps
　　painted, 104, 178
　　paper lanterns, 97
　　pendant, 44, 146
　　proportion and scale, 25
　　shades for, 45, 179
large spaces, 22, 101
lighting, 40–45. See also lamps
　　affordable ideas for, 44
　　amount needed, 43
　　chandeliers, 139
　　natural sunlight, 37
　　types of, 43
living rooms, 59, 64, 65, 83–89

media rooms, 70–79
mirrors, 23, 138, 151
murals, 180–81

nightstands, 156

office spaces, 70–79
orange colors, 36, 79
ottomans, storage, 49

paints, 38–39
photos, enlarging, 88
photos, storing, 49–50
pillows, throw, 74
projects
　　"antique" wicker baskets, 170
　　bark paper ceiling, 176–77
　　chinoiserie mural, 180–81
　　fabric-covered folding screen, 168–69
　　gilded drawer handles, 184–85
　　grid-pattern walls, 186–87
　　no-sew window valence, 166–67
　　padded headboard, 188–89
　　painted lamp, 178
　　stenciled curtains, 174–75
　　striped lamp shades, 179
　　striped walls, 182–83
　　tissue paper walls, 164–65
　　tweed dresser, 171–73
proportion and scale, 20–25
　　beds, 146
　　coffee tables, 77
　　common mistakes, 24–25
　　dining tables, 97
　　matching, 23
　　small consoles, 130
　　windows, 86, 158
purple colors, 36, 133

red colors, 35, 100

screens, folding, 77, 168–69
shelving, 24, 49, 50, 51, 138
sideboards, 104
sinks, bathroom, 51, 112
sitting rooms, 116–27
small spaces, 22. See also apartments

storage solutions
　　banquettes, 109, 141
　　benches, 51
　　cabinet tops, 115
　　faux wall, 138
　　ottomans, 49
　　sideboards, 104
　　Swedish-style buffet, 129

tables
　　bedside, 156
　　clutter on, 125
　　coffee tables, 77, 84
　　dining room, 94, 97, 130, 137–38
　　sideboards and buffets, 104, 129–30
tiles, floor and wall, 112–13
towels, storing, 51

valence, no-sew, 166–67

walls
　　black, 88
　　blue, 110
　　blue-green, 139
　　brown, 157
　　crimson, 100
　　"faux," creating, 138
　　green, 119, 149
　　grid-pattern, 186–87
　　hiding flaws in, 74
　　orange, 79
　　painting mural on, 101–3, 180–81
　　purple, 133
　　striped, 182–83
　　tiles for, 112–13
　　tissue paper, 164–65
　　white, 94
white colors, 35, 94
window treatments
　　curtains, beaded, 137
　　curtains, fabric, 25, 157, 158, 174–75
　　drapes, 25, 93–94, 157
　　no-sew valence, 166–67
　　proportion and scale, 25
windows, 31, 86, 158

yellow colors, 36